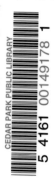

CAREER INTENSITY

Business Strategy for Workplace Warriors and Entrepreneurs

BY
DAVID V. LORENZO

www.careerintensity.com

Permission may be obtained by e-mailing: rights@ogmanpr.com

Published by Ogman Press, Inc
217 East 85th Street
Suite 170
New York, NY 10028

Ogman Press books are available at special quantity discounts for sales promotions, employee premiums, or educational purposes. Please contact the publisher at orders@ogmanpr.com to order.

Publisher's Cataloging-In-Publication Data
(Prepared by The Donohue Group, Inc.)

Lorenzo, David V.
Career intensity : business strategy for workplace warriors and entrepreneurs / David V. Lorenzo.
   p. : ill. ; cm.
Includes bibliographical references and index.
ISBN: 1-933683-00-7
1. Success in business. 2. Career development. I. Title.
HF5386.L67 2006
650.1   2005933518

To my father, Vince Lorenzo, for teaching me my work ethic.

To my mother, Rosemary Lorenzo, for teaching me to be passionate about everything I do.

To Kary for being by my side and giving me the strength to follow my dreams.

TABLE OF CONTENTS

are only effective if they face and defeat their fears. Superachievers know their strengths and weaknesses. They look for opportunities to do what they do best and pursue those opportunities aggressively. They channel their passion into an emotional competitive advantage that makes them unstoppable.

just as a detective focuses when he builds a case. They spend the time necessary to have a solid understanding of the desired outcome of each party in each situation. This preparation allows them to anticipate the needs of the other party and develop a deep and lasting relationship.

they draw a straight line from where they are to where they want to be. They follow that line as a guide toward their dreams, and they let nothing stand in their way.

INTRODUCTION

TAKE CHARGE OF YOUR CAREER

Your career is what happens while you are moving from job to job. Often, you're content to accept your performance reviews and take your cost-of-living increases and move through your career, believing that this modicum of success is the most you can hope for. On those occasions when thoughts creep in that something's missing, you tamp them down and remind yourself to be grateful for what you have. If you're lucky, though, a monumental event wakes you up from your self-induced coma and forces you to realize that there are more opportunities available to you. You can provide more value to the people you serve, you can make more money, and you can have more fun at the same time. My wake-up call came in 2001.

My final job in "my old life" was as a vice president (a title later changed to general manager) of Marriott's ExecuStay brand in New York City. My team and I took a nonexistent business and transformed it into a superstar that outperformed every other unit in the company. We had grown ExecuStay from less than $1 million in annual revenue to over $50 million in just three short years. I often wondered if the business skills I learned there or in any of my other positions during my 15 years in the hospitality industry would translate into success in other industries. Late in 2001, I was given the opportunity to find out.

The events of September 11 were catastrophic to everyone in New York. The loss of the lives of our friends, business partners, and clients was staggering. In the weeks that immediately followed that tragic day, it was impossible to foresee the full impact that the terrorist attacks would have on the economy of New York and of the United States. Once we regained our footing, we began to realize that our business would be hugely impacted by these events. Because ExecuStay was dependent upon relocation and long-term travel to New York, full recovery wouldn't be possible until businesses once again embraced New York City. No one knew how long this would be.

In the immediate aftermath of September 11, our corporate housing business was devastated. Over 30 percent of our apartments were inaccessible due to their proximity to Ground Zero. Within three weeks of the attacks on the World Trade Center, 80 percent of our residents had decided they wanted to live somewhere else. I understood their feelings. We were all worried about the possibility of additional terrorist attacks. The standard rules of business did not apply. We were in uncharted waters.

Faced with the mounting expenses of running a labor-intensive business with a rapidly declining revenue stream, we began to reduce costs. That involved laying off the people who were responsible for our success. In a few short months, we had reduced our staff by two-thirds. At the time, I dwelled on the people who would be out of work and the impact that the layoffs would have on their families.

Once the business was stabilized, I realized that I was at a point where I needed a change. I could no longer come into work every day and face the constant reminder that the business we had built and that was once great had been torn from us. At the same time, I knew that my sadness and anger was nothing compared to the people who had faced the horror of losing a loved one on that terrible day. I recognized that I had an opportunity to do something different with my career. I'd always wondered if the skills and knowledge I had accumulated during my years in the hospitality industry would translate into success in other businesses. In demolishing a business I had helped to build, fate had presented me with the opportunity to find out.

Marriott was a long-time client of The Gallup Organization. In November 2001, I began a dialogue with some of those who were involved in recruiting personnel for Gallup. In early 2002, an opportunity presented itself for me to join the company and lead the startup of the Manhattan Division of The Gallup Organization.

Over the past 20 years, I have taken my business experience and education and applied it to help create a climate of continuous improvement in the projects in which I was involved. During that time, I learned about the determining factors of success in many different industries. As a result, I helped many of these businesses develop processes of continuous improvement that would ensure continued success for the future.

As I reflected upon my own career and how I had been pulled from job to job, it dawned on me that I wasn't following a particular plan. Companies had strategies and continuous improvement models that helped them chart a path toward success, but there was no such model for individuals. I began to focus on the ways in which the factors of business success were applicable to my own career path. I learned to view the world through the eyes of executives and customers in some of the world's best-run organizations. As a result, I formulated and implemented personal strategies of Career Intensity that led to the modest success I now enjoy.

From the moment I made the decision to apply principles of Career Intensity to my own life, I never looked back. They have spurred me to take control of my career and to gain more satisfaction from the work I do.

In the chapters that follow, I've outlined the theory behind Career Intensity and have provided you with actionable strategies to set your own standards of excellence, channel your passion, and create career opportunities. In the process, you'll learn how to create a personal brand that will enhance your career, control others' perceptions of you or your business, and convince others to adopt your ideas.

The first task you face as you read through this book is to decide what resonates with you. Which aspects of your career are you motivated to improve right now? How quickly can you start? If the strategies I've outlined fill you with excitement and enthusiasm, you've already taken a giant step forward. Hope is not a strategy, but it is a fuel that can propel you a long way. The stories and examples provided here are designed to help you picture actual people making a difference in their careers. You should envision yourself in the shoes of those folks. Everyone is different, but we are all human. If they were able to accomplish amazing goals in their careers, then you can too.

If this seems like an emotional appeal, you are correct. As you read on, you will find that emotions play a dramatic role in our lives and in our career successes. You will learn how to look for and leverage the emotions you feel in the decision-making process. You will also learn the value of appealing to the emotions of others in setting a personal marketing strategy and communicating with other people.

Winning over hearts and minds is a phrase that we have heard many times. On your journey, you will learn how to win over the hearts and minds of others. First, though, you need to win the battle for your own heart and mind. Your commitment to make a difference in your own career began when you picked up this book. It will continue on as you work through some of the ideas that I will share with you. You can implement the strategies contained in the suite of tools available at www.careerintensity.com. However, the process must not stop there. It must carry through your entire career.

The most important thing to remember about your career is that every day presents an opportunity to add something new to your personal portfolio. Every day, you have the opportunity to increase your personal equity. If you have the courage to market yourself and the desire to push forward down the path of continuous career improvement, you will be rewarded both financially and intrinsically.

The principles of Career Intensity are applicable whether you're an entrepreneur at heart or are more comfortable working in a corporate setting. You'll find that putting these principles into action will lead to dramatic results. Not only will you manage your own career, but you will also create your own destiny.

Chapter One

COMPETE IN THE INDIVIDUAL ECONOMY

If you reap satisfaction, fulfillment, and financial rewards from your current job, congratulations! If, on the other hand, you feel overwhelmed and undercompensated at work, you're not alone. According to The Conference Board's Consumer Research Center, only half of the working population in the United States expressed satisfaction with their current jobs, and job satisfaction—regardless of income bracket—has been in decline for the past nine years. Similar trends have been noted for the workforces in Europe, Asia, and South America. Much of this dissatisfaction is explained by the increase in demand for individual productivity as a result of rapidly advancing technology.

By taking a strategic approach toward your career development and capitalizing on the shifting focus to individual productivity, your career will continuously increase in value. When you proactively market yourself to your company or clients, the demand for your services will increase. In essence, you will have employed the strategies of the traditional economy to position yourself as a leader in the Individual Economy. Your value to your current employer and to the world at large will increase exponentially, and you will gain an extraordinary amount of career satisfaction, fulfillment, and financial rewards.

SHIFTING LOYALTIES

There are two types of heroes in this world: those who die nobly for a cause and those who live humbly for a cause.

My father is the second kind of hero. He worked for IBM for 40 years and his career was a model of loyalty, persistence, and durability.

Loyalty is an important quality that was instilled in me by my parents. In growing up, my sister and I were taught to be loyal to God, Country, and IBM—in that order. Our family relocated several times so that my father could improve the scope of his career opportunities within the organization. Of course, decisions were always made in the context of what was best for our family, but nary a harsh word was spoken about the company that put the food on the table for so many years.

Twenty years ago, people would have accepted the longevity of my father's career as significant but unremarkable. Such tenure symbolized a solid company that had the interests of its employees at heart. Today, when I tell people about my father's 40 years at IBM, they are astonished. In the twenty-first century, a long career with one company symbolizes the staying power of the individual.

Over the past two decades, we have witnessed a seismic shift in loyalty, in terms of both the loyalty employers show their employees and the loyalty employees feel toward their employers. In effect, both the needs of individuals and the needs of companies have evolved over the years.

The best businesses in every industry are focused not only on how to succeed today, but also on how to sustain growth and profitability for the long term. They realize that what works today may not work tomorrow, and that their currently successful strategy may be their competitor's strategy in the near future. To maintain a competitive advantage, they must have the ability to nimbly move from one approach to another that will be even more effective down the road. Companies live and die by their ability to differentiate from one another and maintain that point of differentiation.

At the same time, the demands thrust on individuals in the corporate world have dramatically increased during the course of the past five decades. As technology advanced the ability to accomplish more with less effort, individuals have been called upon to perform tasks that previously required a team to complete. Processes such as Lean Management, Six Sigma, and Total Quality Management, along with millions of consultants, have streamlined processes to the point where maximum departmental or workgroup productivity can be identified and rapidly replicated. More recently, companies have realized that improvement at the workgroup level is not enough. Improvement or value creation must be taken down to the level of the individual. Throughout this process, the focus has shifted from businesses balancing the needs of their employees against the needs of their bottom lines to a nearly exclusive focus on how the individual can best serve the needs of the company.

Who, then, is ensuring that the needs of the employee are met? Whenever I interview a company executive, I ask him, "Who helps you manage your career and makes certain it is on the right track?" The person whose career has peaked at or below the mid-management level tends to provide an answer that references someone else—human resources, a boss, a mentor, and so on. The highly successful senior manager gives a strikingly different answer—one that reflects an entrepreneurial spirit. He invariably says, "I focus on my own career and development. My future is too important to leave in the hands of someone else."

When it comes to managing their careers, today's successful businesspeople—even those in corporate America—are thinking like entrepreneurs. They don't wait for a roadmap to guide them or for a supervisor to tell them what to do. They work to increase their individual value and differentiate themselves from their competition by staying out in front of the latest initiatives. As a result of their self-analysis, they continuously adjust and improve their performance. In two words, they implement the practice of Career Intensity. In using this approach, they are rewarded with promotions and advancement. In effect, they are building equity in themselves—and that equity is portable. Unlike my father's reciprocal loyalty to IBM, these individuals are committed to the companies for which they work, but their ultimate loyalty is to themselves. This is the reason that, today, a successful individual's 40-year career is likely to include tenure at multiple companies and a personal competitive advantage gained from focusing on value creation through continuous individual improvement.

POSITIONING YOURSELF FOR VALUE CREATION

People in the workforce fall into one of four categories: Workplace Warriors, Management Mavericks, Intrepreneurs, and Entrepreneurs. The individuals who inhabit two of these four categories generate more value than the other two. Entrepreneurs and Intrepreneurs (the two categories above the midpoint line on the Career Intensity Matrix that follows) are the value generators in their organizations.

Career Intensity Matrix

Intrepreneurs	**Entrepreneurs**
Workplace Warriors	**Management Mavericks**

High — Low — High (Value / Risk Tolerance)

Risk Tolerance

There are areas of opportunity for individuals in each of these categories.

Workplace Warrior

The Workplace Warrior is the backbone of any large organization. He can be found in a cubicle or a small, windowless office in every company. He has his head down, and he follows orders. He rarely strays from within his comfort zone, and he measures the worth of his work by a clock, rather than by his accomplishments or growth. In effect, he is grinding it out day-to-day, just doing his job.

While he provides essential services to his organization, the Workplace Warrior is not creating much individual value. He has a perception of job security that comes from the sheer volume of people in his position. In truth, when his company seeks ways to cut expenses through workforce reduction, the Workplace Warrior will feel the brunt of these efforts. With a little training and development of someone else, the Workplace Warrior is replaceable.

His job is also vulnerable to outsourcing. As companies look to become increasingly competitive, Workplace Warriors from emerging nations will take the place of their more expensive peers.

The future is limited for our Workplace Warrior. Although there is still some demand for his services, he needs to take a good, hard look at the future. He must assess his own risk tolerance and the value he can create as an individual. Like everyone, he has the ability to add value to what he offers his company; it is simply a matter of finding the correct opportunity and matching it with his comfort level.

The best place for a Workplace Warrior to begin his self-assessment is to discover his passion. He needs to find an industry that energizes him and determine how he can add value to an existing organization.

Management Maverick

Taking risks is not a problem for the Management Maverick. She has been given this name because of her tendency to move forward and implement solutions without the support of her internal and external customers. Occasionally, this results in a huge success. More often than not, though, she creates an undesirable issue for the company—either internally or externally.

The Management Maverick has a limited future. Frequently, she does not demonstrate significant value to the organization and is perceived as a rogue. Sometimes, she does create value, but it is not understood or recognized. Often, her own perception of the value she is creating is greater than the perceptions of her superiors or customers.

Each of these problems presents the Management Maverick with unique challenges. If she does not demonstrate significant value, she needs to assess both her approach and her performance. She needs to develop a plan for generating value—the sooner the better. Once that plan is in place, she needs to make certain she works on repairing the perception that others in the organization have of her.

If she does create value within her organization and she is not being recognized for her efforts, she must focus on mastering the perception of her internal constituents and external customers. In addition, she should aggressively pursue creating advocates and selling her ideas.

Finally, if her perception of the value she is creating differs from the perception of her internal and external customers, she needs to reassess her choice of employer. Her forward-thinking approach may be too advanced for her current company.

Intrepreneur

The Intrepreneur understands the value he creates within his company. He has a well-defined personal competitive advantage within his peer group. Many times he is the first or the best at critical tasks. He leverages his innate talent to make a difference for his customers. In fact, the Intrepreneur possesses almost all of the qualities of an Entrepreneur, with the exception of risk tolerance. The Intrepreneur prefers to work in a corporate environment.

The future is generally bright for the Intrepreneur, as he often develops new ways to improve the value of his company's business. He should always keep a watchful eye on the market value of his ideas and balance it with his risk tolerance. At some point, he may have an idea or a creative solution with significant market potential that outweighs the risk associated with starting a new business.

An Intrepreneur should always be aware of how he is perceived within his organization. He needs to be careful not to fall into the position of being perceived as a Management Maverick because of his aggressive activity.

The Intrepreneur must also work to develop strong advocates. He must take advantage of his knowledge that the social network in an organization is always more powerful than any form of formal communication. Selling ideas is nothing new for the Intrepreneur. He needs to continue to hone his influence and persuasion skills to make certain that his ideas are always at the top of the list for his internal and external clients.

Entrepreneur

An Entrepreneur is the value creator for her customers. Her high level of confidence in herself and her team affords her a high risk tolerance.

The Entrepreneur has the ability to change or disrupt an entire industry, either locally (the drycleaner who provides same-day service and stays open until 9:00 p.m. to catch the people returning home late from work) or internationally (such as personal computer mavericks Bill Gates and Steve Jobs). This disruption is good for her and creates havoc for her competitors.

Although not essential, creativity is often an important component of the successful Entrepreneur. She is not required to develop new ideas; she specializes in finding new and improved uses for old ideas.

The Entrepreneur is the ultimate re-arranger. She is a master of fighting with the army she has, even if it is not the army she wants. She moves things around to create a business of value to her targeted customer.

She views risk as putting her future in the hands of someone else. The Entrepreneur has faith and confidence in her ability to develop her business.

The Entrepreneur is never as successful as she could be. She views the future as unfulfilled potential. She often has a strong sense of urgency that allows her to get started before actually thinking through the consequences of her actions. This drive also propels her to work long hours, which could potentially lead to burnout or health risks. Balance is critical for the Entrepreneur.

Brand positioning is often missing from the arsenal of the Entrepreneur. Because she generally has a laser-like focus on the operational aspects of her business, she often neglects the process of positioning herself and her products and services.

The Entrepreneur often develops relationships with her customers. The continual nurturing and care of these relationships is critical to creating advocates that will promote her business. An important challenge for the Entrepreneur lies in identifying her high-value customers and converting them into advocates.

A value creator starts as an aggressive, passionate individual who is committed to the success of her career. Her actions are swift and bold. She is decisive and driven to achieve. She is creative and calculating. She combines her skills, knowledge, and talent with a specific strategy that becomes the Career Intensity that propels her to success.

CROSSING THE LINES

To begin to assess the current state of your career, you must identify where you fit into the Career Intensity Matrix. Are you a Workplace Warrior, a Management Maverick, an Intrepreneur, or an Entrepreneur? If you're a Workplace Warrior or Management Maverick, consider the possibility that, deep down inside, you are truly an Intrepreneur or an Entrepreneur. If the timing and the situation were right, could you cross the line and become a value-creating Intrepreneur or Entrepreneur?

Next, review the path you took to the role that you are currently filling at work. When I was 16 years old, I took a job as a dishwasher in an Italian restaurant. This led me to attend culinary school—which led to a degree in hotel/restaurant management—which led to a job in a hotel—which led to a business startup for Marriott—which led to becoming a consultant—which led me back to school—which led me to becoming a strategist—which led me to you. This is not the ideal career path, but it happens to be mine.

If your career path has been similarly circuitous, it's time that you take the reins of your career and begin competing in the Individual Economy. The strategies and tactics I've outlined are designed to help you become an Intrepreneur or an Entrepreneur. Almost all superachievers fall into one of these two categories. These individuals create enormous value for their organizations. As a result, they command a compensation premium over the Workplace Warriors and Management Mavericks.

If you're content remaining in the role of a Workplace Warrior or a Management Maverick, I say that's great. It's difficult to find a job or a career that is rewarding. If your job is meeting your financial needs and exceeding your career aspirations, then you may be in the right role. Keep in mind, though, that you need to be able to look at yourself in the mirror and know that you are reaching your potential. You should also assess the future of your position in your industry. You may be happy where you are, but is your industry happy continuing to do business in its current form?

THE GILLIGAN'S ISLAND THEORY

Years ago, the television show *Gilligan's Island* centered around a group of people who were stranded on a deserted island in the Pacific Ocean. This group of folks was ingenious in finding ways to stay alive and create small comforts while marooned, yet they could not find a way to get off the island. They managed to fight off wild animals, illnesses, storms, and various bad guys, yet they could not find a way to strap some of the trees together and make a boat in order to get home.

Many people have a career that is stuck on Gilligan's Island. They are incredibly creative and valuable individuals. They contribute enormous value to their workgroup and to the company as a whole, yet they never break out and realize their actual worth. They can never get off of the island.

THREE LIES OF CAREER LIMITATION

Most people get into a comfortable career situation and it becomes easy for them to maintain the status quo. As time goes on and they get caught in a tunnel of everyday activity, it becomes increasingly difficult to change. They become blinded to the vast opportunities that the world has to offer. Indeed, they come to believe the Three Lies of Career Limitation:

Security

Lie: My company may not offer me the opportunity to make terrific money or to control my own destiny, but it is a safe and secure place to work. Although my performance is not recognized as outstanding, I can count on having a job to come to every single day.

Truth: The only security you will ever have is confidence in your talent, skills, and knowledge. If you are secure and self-aware, you will always be in demand. Even the most tenured and highest performing employee in a company faces the risk of being fired. The minute a company's profits evaporate, so do the jobs. As we have seen in the cases of Enron, WorldCom, and others, profits can evaporate for a number of reasons that are outside of your control. Security only comes from controlling your own destiny.

Benefits

Lie: I'll never get the (fill in the blank—pay, benefits, time off, tuition reimbursement, free meals) that I have here.

Truth: You can always do better. Outstanding athletes always find a team owner that will pay them more money than did their previous team. You have talent. There is a market for your talent. You simply need to identify your value and your market.

Loyalty

Lie: The company has been good to me all these years. I owe it to them to stay.

Truth: You don't owe anyone anything. Your company is getting a lopsided return on their investment in you. It's guaranteed that you have the potential to generate a minimum of ten times your salary in productivity for your company. If you are not currently doing so, someone is probably going to come and speak with you shortly.

Let's get something straight: I'm not telling you to quit your job and become an entrepreneur. Some people are more comfortable working in the structured confines of the corporate world. What I am advocating is that you take responsibility for your career and focus on improving it. By doing so, you'll provide yourself with more options. You will be able to transfer some of the great creative ideas that you developed while on the island back to the mainland—or to an island of your own.

THE CYCLE OF CONTINUOUS IMPROVEMENT

If you're curious about the impact that this approach to career development can have on your life, you've already taken an important first step. Intellectual curiosity is a necessary prerequisite for success in the Individual Economy.

During a conversation I once had with members of my family, the topic of Australia came up. People were commenting about the length of the journey from New York to the Land Down Under, as well as the beauty of the country. The idea that the seasons were reversed (as compared to the United States) was a topic of great interest. "How did they manage the Olympics?" one person asked. "Can I go skiing there in July?" someone else chimed in. Everyone had a natural curiosity about the differences in style, environment, culture, and so forth.

After listening intently for several minutes, I decided to remark about the more subtle differences that I found fascinating when comparing Australia to the United States. I brought up the topic of water flow in plumbing. You see, legend has it that water flows down the drains (in sinks, bathtubs, etc.) in Australia in the opposite direction of water that drains from plumbing fixtures in the United States. When I brought this up, I immediately recognized the puzzled looks on the faces of my family members as similar to those I had seen in work situations many times over the years. I went on to explain that because of the acceleration associated with the earth's rotation, tropical cyclones (called hurricanes in the Northern Hemisphere) rotate counterclockwise in the Northern

Hemisphere and clockwise in the Southern Hemisphere. Many people assume that this is true of water that flows down drains in household plumbing but it isn't. In household plumbing, the water flows down the drain based upon how it entered the basin in the first place. The shape of the basin will also impact the direction of water flow. I presented this legend and the information that debunked it, to make the point that it is the small differences that make the process of discovery interesting.

In a business setting, we call this process of discovery a situation analysis. When presented with a set of circumstances, we look at the situation on the surface—as the world sees it. Then we dig deeply to find out what is driving that perception.

As people concerned about maximizing the value we provide to our customers, we should frequently conduct a personal situation analysis regarding our careers. To complete this task, we must study our environment, examine our competition, and look for ways we can use our skills, knowledge, and talent to be different.

Looking for the subtle differences in any situation helps me describe my job to people. It's not only the discovery of those subtleties, but also the adaptation of the best discoveries to new situations that often marks the difference between being good and being great.

We should all be dedicated to discovering new things that we can use to improve our careers. This discovery and learning is the first part of the cycle of continuous career improvement. From there, we can apply what we've learned to our careers in a way that makes us different from others in our field. This difference makes us valuable to our customers. Then, we can market ourselves to the world in a way that will help people understand why we are different and how those differences—our ability to generate value— will benefit them. The trick is not to do this once, but to do it in a perpetual cycle—over and over throughout our career.

Personal productivity and value creation through continuous individual improvement are the currency of the Individual Economy. No business can exist without the efforts of the individual employee. Companies are made of workgroups. Workgroups are made up of individuals. Ultimately, the performance of the indi-

The Cycle of Continuous Career Improvement

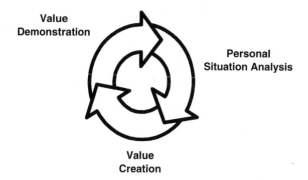

Value Demonstration

Personal Situation Analysis

Value Creation

vidual will determine whether a business will thrive or whether it will dry up and die. Even in an environment that focuses on the performance and productivity of teams, the individuals on the team determine the effectiveness of the team as a whole.

To achieve your goals, you will need to make your career a process of continuous improvement. You must always be willing to look at things from a different perspective. You must be willing to swallow your pride and examine your activities from the perspectives of your boss, your coworkers, and your customers. You need to be able to look in the mirror and ask, "Did I move closer to achieving some of my goals today?" If the answer is "No," you need to decide what you will do differently tomorrow. If you answer that question affirmatively, you need to reflect upon your success and determine how you will exceed it tomorrow.

You career of continuous improvement is a journey. It is not a program from which you graduate. Rather, it is a process that goes on forever. Programs end. A process will never do that.

CREATING VALUE THROUGH GROWTH

Wall Street rewards growth. Companies that consistently show increases in revenue are more valuable than companies that do not.

This is one of the driving principles of business. The greater the growth of the company, the more valuable the firm becomes. Everyone knows, understands, and accepts this fact. Companies are not shy about publicizing their growth rates; in fact, it is required that publicly traded companies do so on a regular basis. When a company perceives that its stock price is too low, it launches massive communications campaigns that are designed to highlight the value the company brings to its customers. These campaigns talk about the competitive advantage the company possesses. They tout the remarkable qualities that set that company apart from its competition. As an individual dedicated to continuous improvement, you must communicate your growth to your customers and potential customers.

Companies set goals. They devise strategic plans that outline the future of the organization. The best firms constantly think about the future. They make decisions within the context of where the company wants to go and understand the implications of each decision. Successful companies conduct significant research before they enter into a business relationship—or even have discussions with other firms. These companies are sales powerhouses. They believe in what they have to offer, and they build persuasive cases to convince others that their offering is compelling. You should be following these same processes in your career.

In fact, all of the operating principles of successful companies also apply to personal growth. As you grow through the acquisition of skills and knowledge (usually measured by education and experience), your value increases. You should be able to follow all of the principles of successful companies and increase your value, just as a company increases its value. You should manage your career the way a company manages its position in the market.

In many companies, there is no equity between employee compensation and value creation. It is just not practical for firms to pay individual employees in that fashion. Instead, companies look at job classifications and benchmark against the compensation provided by other organizations for that job classification. This is the system that most organizations feel provides the fairest compensation to individuals for their services.

Now comes the true question: Why must those individuals who provide outstanding value be subject to the same (or similar) compensation standards as everyone else? In short, they shouldn't. Individuals who provide outstanding value can challenge the system and win. Their commitment to continuous improvement— their Career Intensity—helps them catapult themselves beyond the proscribed systems that the corporate world has set for them.

GAINING ADVANTAGE THROUGH PERSISTENCE

Eddie Cantor, a star of stage, screen, radio, and TV from 1904 to 1960, famously said, "It took me twenty years to become an overnight success." Let's think about that literally. If I told you today that your dreams would come true if you gave 100 percent effort every day toward those dreams for the next 20 years, would you be able to do it? Let's say that you could make a fine living and you would be comfortable, but that you had to give 100 percent of your effort toward your dream each eight-hour workday, five days a week, for the next 20 years. Would you be able to sustain that type of effort to accomplish your most fantastic ambition? What if it took 10 years? Could you maintain your persistence over the long haul?

Persistence—sustained effort in the face of adversity—is exactly what it takes to realize your dreams. You will have incremental successes along the way that will help to keep you motivated. Ultimately, though, the will to keep going will be the most critical aspect of your success.

As you begin looking at ways to enhance your career, you must be persistent in your desire to improve.

How many times have you missed an appointment, a party, or an event, only to have someone tell you that it was fantastic? I want you to remember the feeling you have when you discover that you missed out. You should feel that way right now about your career. At this very moment, great things are happening for other people. What is the difference between you and them? They are present. They show up. They engage themselves in the process of making their careers better each and every day. The value of showing up each day—in body, mind, and spirit—cannot be overstated. You need to break through obstacles and keep showing up.

My interaction with successful people over the years has helped me to understand that persistence can pay off not only in the end result, but also in the journey. There is a story that I tell about persistence that helps put things in perspective for many people. I call it "The New York Advantage," and it is all about the persistence that you can develop by facing adversity on a regular basis.

When you live in New York City, you face adversity every day. Survival of the fittest is the code of the urban jungle in New York. Imagine awakening in the morning and walking several blocks in the hot sun to the subway. It appears as if you never have enough room on the sidewalk, because there are always about a dozen people going in your direction—but at a much slower pace. There are also twice as many people coming the other way—walking directly toward you, giving you a look that says, "I will knock you over and clean my shoes on your hair as I pass by."

After you jockey your way down into the subway, you rub very vulnerable parts of your body against complete strangers just to find a place to stand on the subway platform. By 7:00 a.m., it's about 95 degrees on the platform. You have already sweated through your undershirt, and you have resorted to holding your jacket over your arm—and you think you look good.

The train comes and you elbow someone to get into the car just before the doors close. As you turn to hold the metal bar to steady yourself, you notice a man in what appears to be a minister's collar rubbing his eye back on the platform. As the train pulls away, he looks up and gives you the finger.

You only need to ride the subway a couple of stops to get to the office, but the train is crawling along more slowly than you can walk because other trains are ahead of you. Your eyes are focused on the ceiling or on the floor because if you make eye contact with anyone, you will definitely get punched in the mouth. As you look at your shoes, you think you may have stepped in something on the walk to the subway because you smell an unpleasant odor. You glance up, ever so briefly, and you realize that your nose and mouth are about three inches away from the armpit of a man who has obviously worked the nightshift near a blast furnace. Then you realize you are sweating as much as he is.

You finally get to your stop, and you again go through the uncomfortable rubbing routine, and maybe you throw another elbow to get out of the subway car. Then you jostle and shove onto the escalator to get out of the station. When you finally make it to daylight, you realize what a beautiful day it is and how lucky you are to live in the greatest city in the world. You feel this way because you know that anyone who is not from New York could not understand the mentality that is necessary to survive here. Just the ride to work in the morning would be enough to send most people to another town.

That's the New York Advantage. The fundamental ingredient is persistence, the ability to overcome adversities large and small. Life pushes us; we push right back. If you put something in the way, we throw an elbow. You knock our buildings down, we bury our dead, honor our heroes, and we come looking for you. We will be twice as strong as we were before. That's the attitude you need to have toward life. That is the attitude that separates successful people from the rest of the world.

I do not mean to imply that only people from New York can be this persistent. I am merely using New York as an example of the type of resolve necessary to achieve sustainable success. Going to work in Omaha, Des Moines, Mumbai, Rio de Janeiro, or any other place each and every day can be just as challenging—especially if you do not feel that you make a difference. You can develop an attitude that helps you appreciate the value you provide in your work. You will be able to market that value to everyone around you in a nonthreatening way that draws people closer to you. To do this, you need to challenge yourself at every opportunity. Stare every adversity in the face and put 100 percent of your effort toward defeating it. Just the act of continuing on, in spite of long odds and even significant setbacks, will make you stronger each day. You should pride yourself on your ability to overcome obstacles. They are opportunities for you to become stronger. Take a look around you at work and in other aspects of life. Have you seen people give up on great ideas just because the journey was difficult or because the hurdles were too high? The most precious asset each one of us possesses is our potential. Wasting potential is more shameful than wasting money. You are about to unleash your potential upon the world by taking control of your career.

Chapter Two

CHANNEL YOUR PASSION

That knot or sinking feeling in the pit of your stomach that you feel on Sunday night as you look ahead to another week at work and the dread that envelopes you as you perform the mundane tasks that fill your days at the office are the career equivalent of flashing red lights. They are sure signs that you haven't discovered and channeled your passion—that you haven't taken the steps necessary to move toward your goals and achieve your dreams.

When you assume responsibility for your career, you will move into the driver's seat and take control of your destiny. When you overcome the fears that keep your career stuck in neutral, you can accelerate toward your goals. When you clearly understand the impact of your decisions and actions, you have a roadmap to success. Ultimately, you become driven by an unstoppable force that is, in essence, Career Intensity.

Once you have made the commitment to value creation through the process of continuous improvement, you are on your way to becoming an intense, driven person who will stop at nothing until you are living your dream. At this point, you must carefully exorcise the self-doubt that will drive your career into a ditch.

You will achieve all of your goals. It will happen. Whenever a doubt creeps into your mind, you need to banish it as if it were the enemy. Doubt is the enemy of success. As long as you have the ability to draw breath, you have the ability to achieve your goals. You are smart enough and you have as much ability to become successful as anyone else.

To reinforce this thinking, get a rubber band and put it around your wrist. Any type of rubber band will do. Now, when you find yourself daydreaming about your goals or your future success and a doubt creeps into your thoughts, snap the rubber band. When you feel the sting, tell yourself that self-doubt can only hurt your progress and that, as you move forward, there is no room for it in your life. Immediately think about a positive action you can take to make your daydream a reality. The trick is to associate pain with the negative thought and replace it immediately with a positive image. Practice this exercise for a week or until you find yourself immediately replacing negative thoughts and self-doubt with possibilities.

Your mind has the ability to create any world that you can imagine. Perspective is simply the way you see things, and not necessarily the way they really are. The first step in developing Career Intensity lies in taking control of your own mind by controlling your thoughts. It's your responsibility.

Taking Control Through Assuming Responsibility

Your life is a sum of your experiences, and you have the ability to impact every experience. Yes, you can have an impact on each and every experience in your life. People often say, "There was nothing I could do" or "I was a victim of circumstance." Those are statements made by people who do not want to control their own destinies. Each one of us has the ability to control how we react to challenging situations. It is critical that you take immediate responsibility for your own future. Every action you take involves a choice. Take a deep breath and assume responsibility for your future.

When I talk about assuming responsibility for the future, often someone will describe a situation that appears to be out of her control, such as a car accident. It is true that things happen to all of us that cannot be foreseen, let alone prevented. Yet, there is still an element of the situation that we do control. In the face of adversity, we control our reaction to that challenge. No matter what the situation, each of us has the ability to control our reaction. One person may allow the adversity of a difficult situation to drive her down a path of negativity. Another will use adversity as an opportunity to become stronger. In each case, the individual made a choice.

Taking responsibility begins with giving up the drudgery of everyday tasks that you hate. It means leaving the temporary job that has become your career. The assumption of responsibility should empower you to shape your destiny. I often ask people the question, "If money were not an issue for you but you needed to be employed, what would you be doing?" Most people respond with occupations that are dramatically different than their current positions. When I ask a person why he doesn't move into the role he desires, his answer is often related to his financial situation. I then ask, "If you had a plan to move into that occupation and make more money doing it, but that plan took a year to execute, would you do it?" His answer is always, "Yes!" Even if I extend the question to reflect a five- or ten-year period, he will often respond affirmatively.

The point of this line of questioning is to help him understand where his true passion lies. Successful people begin to take responsibility for their future by following their passion and making their passion their career. People who are passionate about what they do often find that the time they spend at work passes very quickly. Instead of feeling drained at the end of their workday, they are energized by what they have accomplished. On a Sunday night, they feel a sense of anticipation toward the week ahead. They are driven by an almost unstoppable force that gives them the energy and enthusiasm that infects everyone they meet during the course of their workday. Assuming responsibility is the key to unlocking this power. Assume responsibility for each and every action you take. Start by assuming responsibility for your career.

THE FIVE IRRATIONAL FEARS

As human beings, we all experience fear. Fear is an emotion that evolved as a form of protection from painful or possibly fatal situations. Rational fears protect us. Healthy fear keeps us from acting in ways that would put our lives in danger. It keeps us from walking into a lion's den or placing our hands in a roaring fire. On the other hand, we develop irrational fears as the result of painful past experiences and conjure them up when we anticipate a similar negative experience. Irrational fears can hold us back and steal our dreams.

To help overcome irrational fear, many people use a great acronym that places it in the proper context. **FEAR** is **F**alse **E**vidence **A**ppearing **R**eal. People with Career Intensity—Intrepreneurs and Entrepreneurs—have discovered ways to overcome the Five Irrational Fears that prevent people from creating their own destiny:

The fear of the unknown. You don't know what the future will bring. You may know that greater possibilities exist, but what you have now is familiar. It's difficult to give up the certainty of the familiar for the uncertain rewards of the unfamiliar.

This major hurdle is usually associated with income and is the fear that prevents most people from taking action. A few years ago, I was having lunch with a business leader I know and respect. This man was a partner in a very successful real estate development firm in New York City. During the course of our lunch, the topic of forming my own business came up. The developer asked me why I was working for a large company when I clearly had the talent to go out on my own and start a business. I responded that the timing was not right. His response comprised the truest words I have ever heard on this topic. He said, "There is never a good time. If you wait for a good time, you will never get going. You just have to face up to whatever concerns you and move forward."

He was right. I waited a few more years and a good time never presented itself. I needed to just move forward and not look back. It was (and sometimes still is) scary, but the only way to make things happen is to face the fear and plow ahead—without looking back.

The fear of failure. What if the change you make isn't for the better? What will people think of you? People will laugh at you if you fail, and you'll be embarrassed.

A great way to approach this fear is to reflect upon successful people who have had very public failures and still managed to recover. One of my favorite examples concerns the repeated public failures of Abraham Lincoln. Lincoln lost his job as a clerk in a general store in 1831. He ran for the Illinois state legislature in 1832 and lost. In 1843, he failed to win his party's nomination for a congressional seat. He tried running for the Illinois Senate in 1854. He lost. In 1858, he unsuccessfully ran for the U.S. Senate again. After each of those defeats, people laughed at Lincoln, yet in 1860, he was elected the 16th president of the United States. He has become one of history's most respected figures. Most people do not know about his previous failures or that people laughed at him each time. Somehow, I do not think people were laughing at him when he gave the Gettysburg Address.

The lesson to be learned is that history will be the ultimate judge of your success. You should not fear failure; each time you fail, you are taking another step closer toward success.

The fear of commitment. Like each of us, you have a strong desire to do what you say you are going to do. The psychological need for your actions to match your words drives you to follow through on whatever commitments you make. That type of commitment implies hard work, and you'd rather not commit than compromise your integrity by failing to keep your word. This is especially true when you make a commitment to yourself.

The psychology of commitment is a mental Catch-22. Your impulse to keep your word—make your commitment come true— is so great that it causes you to avoid making commitments.

There are two ways to overcome this fear of commitment. The first is to contrast possibility with probability. If it is probable that you will accomplish the task at hand, then you should be able to make the commitment. For example, if you are asked to take on a job with tight deadlines and you are afraid that you will be unable to meet the deadlines, you may be reluctant to take the job. In reflecting on your work history, you can only think of one time when you did not meet a deadline—and that was due to the death of a family member. In this case, then, it is possible that you will miss deadlines, but based on your track record, it is not probable.

The second way to tackle this fear is to view a large commitment as a series of smaller commitments. This is the one-day-at-a-time philosophy that has proved so successful in helping people break addictions. Your short-term concern is meeting your goal today. Before you know it, your days turn into months and your months turn into years. Each day of success becomes positive reinforcing behavior. In the process, the basis of your fear becomes familiar and is no longer a threat.

The fear of disapproval. Other people may not like the change you've made, even if that change improves your life. When it comes to making a change, gaining approval can be the wind in your sails. When people who are important to you are skeptical or disagree with you, you feel like you are running uphill.

When we were kids, we all craved the approval of our parents and the elders in our social environment. People who grow up never gaining the approval of their parents (or other influential individuals) can often have a fear of disapproval that will limit their career progression.

When I was in culinary school, I had a classmate named Jessica who baked beautiful cakes. She was a naturally talented pastry artist. Jessica's cakes would often be entered into contests and she would almost always win one of the prizes. This was quite ironic because Jessica did not score well on the practical exams the school gave to students as they finished their training. When I asked Jessica how she could do so well in the contests and then so poorly on the exams, her answer gave me my first exposure to the negative power of the fear of disapproval.

She told me that, in the contests, she was just baking for herself. She was trying to make the best product she could. The feedback she received was direct and without detail. Either she was a winner or she was not.

In class, the instructors always found something wrong with her work. In an exam, even if she received an "A," she would be given feedback that told her what she could have done better. This fear of negative feedback—of disapproval—led her to try to make everything perfect in the short period of time that she had to complete the work for the exam. It was an impossible task, and one that reinforced her core fear.

Successful individuals are confident in their ideas and don't require outside validation. In fact, they are motivated to prove others wrong. Because superachievers are unique, it is no surprise to them when others do not approve of their actions or their ideas. Intrepreneurs and Entrepreneurs typically don't take conventional paths toward their goals. When you stray from the conventional or the familiar, you are likely to draw some curiosity—and some disapproval—from others. At the end of the day, though, the only person you have to answer to is yourself. You owe yourself every opportunity to succeed. If you let an opportunity pass you by because you are concerned about the disapproval of another person, you are robbing yourself. You can't let someone else determine your fate.

The fear of success. As much as you want to be the best, you're afraid that if you actually achieve more, others will dislike you, shun you, and think you're arrogant. You may also feel that the pressure of being successful may be too great a load to bear or that you will never live up to the expectations of others.

It is true that it is easier to get to the top than it is to stay on top. This is partially due to increased competition and increased expectations that come along with success. However, the rewards of high achievement far outweigh the burden of the duty and responsibility associated with staying there.

People who dislike you when you attempt to control your own career destiny are not your friends. They might say things like, "You have a perfectly good job now" or "Why are you wasting your time with a book or learning program?" The best approach to take with a naysayer is to understand her motivations. First, mediocrity loves company. Deep down, insecure people resent the success of others in their peer group. Your success only highlights their mediocrity. Second, as you move toward your career goals, you may have less in common with those who do not take control of their own destiny. They may sense this and push you away. Third, your focus on self-improvement may temporarily shift your focus away from the attention you have previously given to other people, which causes them to resent you.

How you handle these individuals is entirely up to you. I prefer to thank my friends and relatives for their concern and then continue on with my aggressive pursuit of success. Once the people who really care about me gain a sense of how success has changed my life, they become supportive.

The fear of success is often rooted deep in the subconscious mind of the Workplace Warrior and the Management Maverick. More often than not, a person's fear of success has its genesis in a defining moment that occurred while he was growing up.

Not too long ago, I met a warm, engaging sales representative named Rick. Rick was an outstanding account manager. His position was that of inside sales, a role that required the sales representative to make phone calls to prospective clients and ask for business. Rick was also great at some of the local networking events the company attended in its city.

Rick's performance earned him the next step in the natural career progression at this company—a promotion to account executive. The account executive role in this particular organization was a position that had similar requirements to the account manager position; the only difference was that the actual sales process was conducted in person. The account executives traveled to meet with their clients several times each month.

Rick's manager asked me to speak to Rick because he was not performing well as an account executive. He had only contracted business with five new companies in the past three months and his activity (the number of meetings he attended with clients) was light.

After speaking with Rick a few times, I learned that his father was a highly successful sales representative in the professional tool industry. Rick fondly said that sales was in his blood. However, he was visibly upset when he talked about the negative aspect of his father's career—that his father was on the road quite a bit when he was young. I also learned that, around the same time as he had received the promotion to account executive, Rick and his wife had welcomed a baby boy into their family.

After much discussion and some deep soul searching, Rick realized that he was afraid to succeed in his role. He believed that success would require more travel and that in traveling, he would be neglecting his wife and baby. This fear caused him to focus exclusively on accounts that he could service with a day trip in order for him to be home each evening.

Rick was able to address his fear by having a deep conversation with his wife. They agreed that Rick would give 100 percent of his effort in his new job for two years. During this time, he would do everything necessary to succeed. If Rick were not promoted to a management position after the second year, he would ask to be moved into a different role—one that required no travel.

Placing an end date on the driver of the fear helped Rick overcome his subconscious fear of success. The support of his wife allowed him to give himself permission to be successful.

Because irrational fears are learned, you can "unlearn" them by changing your thought process. Using the same principle as the rubber band exercise discussed earlier, every time you catch yourself thinking about the "negative consequences" of success, immediately change your thought pattern. For example, when you think that if you are successful, your friends will perceive you as arrogant, you should immediately recognize this as a self-limiting thought. Then you can unlearn the fear by thinking, "It is possible but not probable that people will perceive me as arrogant, but that will only happen if I allow my behavior toward my friends to change. I will be successful, and I will not change my behavior toward my friends. I control my behavior and my reactions. My success will actually allow me to spend more time with my friends."

Preparing for success is the best way to overcome both your conscious and unconscious fears. Each day, you should spend time visualizing the new successful you. Imagine your success in as much detail as possible. If you aspire to be a successful executive in a company—an Intrepreneur—picture yourself in a big chair in a large corner office. Imagine your friends coming in and out to see you. If your dream is to open a wildly successful business as an Entrepreneur, imagine all of your employees lining up to shake your hand because you have created a company that has transformed their lives.

When you use this visualization process, you are actually participating in a form of exposure therapy. Your unconscious mind does not make a distinction between imagination and reality, so when you imagine yourself as a rich, successful executive, your mind starts getting used to the image. The more you expose yourself to a situation you fear, the less potent the fear becomes. You should use visualization several times a day to help you overcome any conscious or unconscious fear you may have that will hold you back on your journey to fulfill your dreams.

Developing a Mental Training Regime

We have all heard the expression, "It don't come easy" in reference to success. This is the truth. Although success may appear to happen in an effortless fashion, someone somewhere worked very diligently behind the scenes to ensure optimal results. You must prepare your mind for the difficult tasks that lay ahead of you as you drive your way toward success. Just as a world-class athlete spends years training his body to take the punishment of intense competition, you must train your mind for the battles you will face on the road to making your goals a reality.

Your mental training regime involves challenging yourself with completing increasingly difficult tasks that require you to be alone. The task, be it an intellectual pursuit like getting a degree, or an artistic pursuit like painting or writing poetry, will help you push your limits and develop the mental toughness you need to become a success.

You will learn more about yourself during this strenuous alone time than you would after hours spent on a psychologist's couch. When you focus your alone time on really difficult tasks, you battle every vice you have. When you win these battles, you gain the confidence that comes with self-awareness. You will know how far you can push yourself, knowledge that is absolutely critical to your career success.

Education is a great activity to boost your confidence, and it fits the criteria of something that is difficult and something you must do alone. When I decided to pursue a career in consulting, I felt that I needed to broaden my background and add some business theory to the knowledge base I had developed through experience. At the age of 34, I decided to return to school and pursue an MBA. It had been 13 years since I was last in a classroom—and I was not an outstanding student when I earned my undergraduate degree. My experience in earning my MBA was enlightening, but not just because of the knowledge I acquired. This experience taught me that I had enormous capacity for time management, project prioritization, and mental fortitude. There was a short ramp-up period where I had to adjust to the additional workload, similar to the soreness you feel when you begin a physical workout program for the first time. I experienced a kind of mental soreness as I figured out how to shift my priorities and get everything done.

Once I got past the mental soreness, I learned that I had the capacity to do more. In the second year of working on my MBA, I was accepted to Columbia University. Columbia offers a masters degree in strategic communications, a topic that always interested me. During the second year of my MBA program, I began my first year at Columbia—all while working full-time. It was through this experience that I learned how far I could push myself mentally. I continue to be amazed at the capacity we all possess for growth and improvement. The pursuit of both of these degrees—solitary and time-intensive efforts—helped shape my thinking for the difficult tasks that lie ahead as I move forward in life.

Outcome-Driven Thinking

Successful people approach their every interaction in a manner that's different than everyone else. People who are successful enter into each interaction with a desired outcome. They have an idea of what they want from each meeting, each phone call, and each e-mail. The most successful individuals have internalized this behavior; they don't even realize that they are doing it. There is also a flip side to this coin. Successful people are incredibly appreciative when other people are focused on achieving an outcome from a meeting or interaction. This helps them cut through clutter and enables them to be almost twice as productive as everyone else.

Many people ask me if, by outcome-driven, I mean communicating in a frank or direct way. Although direct communication is often helpful and appreciated, that is not my specific focus. In this case, I am referring to the thought process that occurs prior to an interaction, such as scheduling a meeting, accepting an invitation to a meeting, picking up the phone, writing an e-mail, or even going to the store. Most people take these things for granted. You will sit in a meeting for an hour or more and then leave the room wondering why you just wasted an hour of your life. You go to the mall with no clear purpose and end up just killing time.

Outcome-driven thinking is about being in the moment. What you do right now will create your past and it will have an impact on your future. Your life is a collection of these finite opportunities. You do not know when they will run out, so you owe it to yourself to make the most out of each and every moment. Entertainers say that when you go up onstage, you have to "be in the room." You need to be in tune with everything that is going on around you and act in harmony with those events. You have to be present in order to make a difference. In business, use these moments to advance toward the outcome you seek. Take advantage of the fact that you have that critical person on the phone, or that he reads your e-mail at the beginning of the day. Use these tools to your advantage.

Giving thought to the desired outcome in each situation will do three things for you:

> **You will not enter into time-wasting activities.** If you cannot identify the outcome for a potential meeting, you should not go. If you can't identify the specific outcome for a phone call you have scheduled, don't make the call.
> **You will prioritize important activities.** Let's face it: Some things are more important than others. If you have taken the time to identify what you hope to accomplish with each and every interaction, you will be able to choose which things you should handle yourself and which things you can allow others to handle.

You will make better decisions. Once you internalize outcome-driven thinking, you think better on your feet. Your mind will instantly (eventually subconsciously) think about the outcome of a potential situation, and you will be able to react more quickly than others.

Being in the moment and focusing on outcomes means taking a quality vs. quantity approach to the way you live your life and conduct your business. I once interviewed a great sales manager I'll call Bob. Bob took over the floundering division of a copier company and, in less than a year, turned it into the company's most profitable division. His progress was staggering. When I met with him to learn about the secret of his success, Bob said that the key was his system for tracking sales activity and using that tracking system as a coaching tool. His system was a great illustration of quality vs. quantity in outcome-driven thinking.

Bob said, "I ask each sales rep to list out the meetings they had for the past week. Then I ask them what they hoped to accomplish in that meeting and what they actually accomplished. The catch is that I ask them what they hope to accomplish in next week's meetings, too. We then compare the expectations to the actual outcomes from each meeting and discuss next steps based upon those outcomes."

When I asked Bob if this was time-consuming, he replied, "The first few weeks were difficult. Some of the reps had 15 or more meetings in a five-day workweek. These were incredibly unproductive meetings. We began calling them 'hit-and-run' meetings. By the third week, even the most ambitious rep was down to eight meetings, max. The outcomes were much more refined and specific, and the result was more closed deals."

In the case of Bob and the copier sales team, higher quality meetings resulted in more deals. Bob forced his people to think about the desired outcome before they ever went to the meeting. To understand how Bob's system transformed a low-performing team into all-stars, I interviewed a woman named Jennifer. She was in the bottom 10 percent in the country in sales before Bob took over as her manager. One year later, she was recognized as the top performer in their Northeastern Sales Region. She said that Bob's outcome-based activity system was instrumental for her success. "Focusing on an outcome before going on a meeting really forced me to thoroughly prepare for each meeting. It also kept me on track while I was at the meeting. I knew that if I did not get accomplished what I wanted to at each meeting, I would not make my goals. This created an internal pressure that has been the driving force in my success."

Making certain that you know what you want from each activity in your life makes sense. Beyond that, it is critical that this type of thinking become second nature. If you can internalize outcome-driven thinking, you will immediately double your productivity in business and have a more rewarding career.

HARNESSING YOUR IMAGINATION

Your imagination is a powerful tool that you should leverage in mapping out your future. As previously discussed, your mind does not differentiate between what is real and what is imagined. There are three ways you can use your imagination as you begin your program of continuous improvement.

- Consciously shape your daily activities to move you closer toward your goals.
- Make changes in your environment that will influence you—on conscious and unconscious levels—to focus on your goals.
- Behave as though you have already achieved your goals.

Even though fear embedded in the unconscious mind can sabotage our success, the reverse is also true. You can use your unconscious mind to influence your thinking in order to achieve your goals. This is an incredibly powerful process that all successful individuals have mastered. Many of these people were unaware that they had actually "programmed" themselves for success; in reality, they had shaped their destiny deep within their unconscious minds long before reaping their rewards.

Essentially, this process involves acting as if you have already met the goal or assumed the position you would like to achieve. As an example, in 1996, I met Don, the general manager of a small hotel in Westchester County, New York. He was one of the top general managers in his company. His financial results were second to none and his customers and employees all liked and respected him. His personal appearance was clean-cut and low-key. He had a great sense of humor and made people feel at ease. Don was a likable and generous person who was always willing to share advice with his peers. In fact, Don would go out of his way to help other hotel managers in his company who were struggling. He would often spend his own time working with the general manager of a sister hotel to improve her property. Don did all of this work through his own initiative and, most of the time, without the knowledge of his boss. He was also outstanding at developing his own people. When he would leave his hotel for weeks at a time to work with other managers, his property would not miss a beat. His assistant general manager was well trained and was one of the most competent people in her field. She was often recognized as a great leader in her own right.

In 1998, Don was promoted to a regional manager position. I met up with him at a conference and asked him how his job had changed. He described some of the new branding initiatives he was developing for the company. He talked about how he had volunteered to work on some franchisee-related projects and on the owner services team at corporate. He also told me how proud he was that he had trained the general managers in his region, now his subordinates, to help one another solve problems. He said that property inspections were more like visits with friends because things were running so smoothly.

Don's story is a clear example of "Acting as if . . ." In his role as a general manager, Don was already acting as if he were a regional manager. When the time came to promote someone, Don's superiors and his peers not only recognized his ability, but they naturally gravitated toward him as the perfect choice. In his role as the regional manager, Don was already volunteering for responsibilities that would help him prepare for a role at the corporate office—the next step in his career progression.

Further, Don's focus on developing his subordinates was key. He learned early on that, in order to "Act as if . . ." he needed to make certain he had people on board that would act as if they were in his position. Don had already assumed the mindset he would need in his future role and knew that developing the people under him was critical to his success.

The first step in changing your mindset and moving toward a new position, or a new career, is to understand what is involved in the new role. For example, if you want to start a business, you should interview people who have started businesses that are similar. You will gain an understanding of their thought processes and behaviors. Observe them in action. See what they do and how they do it. Spend as much time in that environment as possible. Think about what you would do differently.

For example, let's say that you want to become the owner of a McDonald's franchise. Stop in your local McDonald's and talk with the manager. Ask her what she likes about working there. Ask her what she thinks could be improved. Ask if you can contact the owner and speak with him. Ask him to tell you his success story. More often than not, people are happy to share their stories with you. Not only are you gaining information to prepare for an ownership role in the future, but you are also programming your unconscious mind to believe that you are already in that position.

Next, you should surround yourself with items that symbolize what you hope to become. If you want to become a McDonald's franchise owner, cut out some photos of a McDonald's restaurant and tape them to your wall. Read books about McDonald's. Imagine your success in this role. If owning several of these restaurants will make you rich enough to buy a boat, put some pictures of boats up on your wall, too.

Finally, before you go to sleep at night and immediately upon waking in the morning, think about what your day would be like if you achieved this new position. As you fall asleep, imagine yourself counting your money with the manager who works for you. Imagine, in vivid detail, taking the briefcase full of money to the marina and purchasing your boat. Then, when you wake up the next day, imagine how your day would start if you owned that restaurant. Imagine pulling into the parking lot and seeing it full of cars. Imagine a counter packed with a line of happy customers being served by employees who smile and nod as you walk into the building.

The more you practice this process of acting as if you were in the role you seek, the more natural your transition into that role will become. You should not limit yourself to small dreams. Successful people acted in ways appropriate to the roles they would assume years before they achieved their success. When they got there, they felt and behaved as if they had been doing it all their lives.

Chapter Three
EMBRACE STRATEGIC THINKING

Have you ever had a moment when you wished for a second chance at a decision, when you clearly recognized that you had acted irrationally? Virtually everyone has had 20/20 hindsight at some point in their lives and has longed for the opportunity to revisit a critical decision. The failure to think strategically—to see a clear path through the mental haze that surrounds a decision—when faced with a career-related or life-changing choice can mean the difference between rousing success and dismal failure. If you aspire to greatness, the process of strategic thinking must become second nature to you. By examining the implications of your choices and analyzing the options available to you before you make decisions, you will develop a competitive advantage in business and in life.

In its highest form, strategic thinking is a distinct perspective that helps you break down complicated processes into easily manageable pieces that can be arranged to present a clear set of alternatives. Some people are blessed with a unique perspective that allows them to mentally break down complex issues and picture alternatives with ease. Others must learn this type of behavior. The process of learning to think strategically is similar to learning a foreign language. As an American born and raised in New York, I learned to speak Spanish in my late twenties. As I practiced speaking Spanish, I became better and better at thinking and responding in a language that was not native to me. Today, I have internalized the language to the point where my response time in Spanish is equal to my response time in English; however, speaking Spanish requires significantly more effort than speaking my native language. Those who are natural strategic thinkers can intuitively develop alternatives to complex issues once they review the existing evidence or data. People who learn strategic thinking can also achieve the same result—it just might take more time and effort. A superachiever brings intensity to his thinking process. He is intellectually curious and aggressive. In his individual cycle of continuous improvement, he thinks like a well run company—strategically. He thinks several moves ahead in his career. He embraces the future as if it were an old friend whose return he has anticipated for months.

SABOTAGING SOUND DECISION MAKING

Your mind has three interrelated and interdependent functions: reasoning, feeling, and wanting. The three act together in your thinking process and each contributes to the decisions that you make. Often, your most powerful emotions and desires are not apparent to your conscious mind. These influential subconscious feelings and desires can often be irrational, senseless, or not follow a coherent flow. I'm not talking about the way in which wearing a lampshade on your head at a party is irrational. I am talking about everyday decisions that you make without the benefit of solid, logical thinking.

Ron's experience is a perfect example of irrational decision making. He is a talented midlevel executive for a retail company, which he joined five years ago. The company is a small, family-run business that has not grown significantly in three years. His career is now stagnating because there are few positions into which he can be promoted. This particular company has always placed members of the owning family in the senior executive roles.

Ron knows he has the talent and skill to run a company one day. In the past, he was a regional manager for two well-respected national organizations, and he has launched two profitable divisions for his current company. In order to advance his career, it is critical that Ron obtain executive experience in finance. Ron knows this, and so he contacts several executive recruiters and asks them to add his name to the list of candidates for executive positions. He goes on three interviews over the course of a month, but no job offers materialize.

After the third interview, Ron becomes discouraged and begins to believe that he does not have what it takes to land an executive finance position. He feels that additional interviews will only confirm this fact. Ron decides to call off the search and remain in his current role.

With this decision, Ron has given up on the potential of an incredibly rewarding career—a career he has dreamed of pursuing—because three companies rejected him. Those three companies make up an infinitesimal proportion of the thousands of retail organizations in the nation where he could succeed. Ron's discouragement has driven a change in his behavior that will have a profoundly negative effect on his entire career.

If he were to think about this situation logically, Ron would realize that he could be a viable candidate for hundreds of potential positions. His résumé is strong and he interviews well. It will take time to find the right fit, but eventually, he will find the position he needs. The pain of rejection is a temporary situation that will pass, but in the midst of his discouragement, Ron abandons his career ambitions.

This happens to all of us. Your emotions influence your thinking on a subconscious level. You may not even be aware that this is happening, yet you make plans or decisions based upon this irrational thinking.

FIVE FACTORS THAT INFLUENCE STRATEGIC THINKING

Strategic thinking involves both the rational and the emotional functions of the brain. When someone with Career Intensity makes plans, solves problems, or makes decisions in either her personal or professional life, she relies on both aspects of thought. Most often, these top performers do not realize they are thinking emotionally or rationally; they just know that they make good decisions, that they plan well, or that they are great problem solvers. There are five factors that influence the thinking of superachievers: time, control, experience, the unknown, and outcome finality. None address the personal stake the individual has in the outcome. This is because every plan, every decision, or every problem you work on is personal. You are emotionally invested in the outcome of the situation. There are different degrees of emotional investment which may make some decisions appear more personal than others. It is impossible to remove emotion from your life. So you must move forward with the knowledge that everything is personal to some degree—that all situations have an emotional aspect to them. Any belief to the contrary is simply denial.

When making a decision, a top performer's first step is to acknowledge the factor that most influences the process. When telling a story about a critical decision or a well-developed plan, he will say something like, "We knew we had limited time" or "We knew we could not control the competitor's response." Failing to acknowledge a factor that may have an influence on a situation will almost always result in an unwelcome surprise. Let's take a look at the five factors and their potential impact on the strategic-thinking process.

Time

The first question asked by a strategic thinker is, "How much time do I have to develop this plan, make this decision, or solve this problem?" This is the factor that will have the most influence on how the individual will proceed. Almost every other aspect of solution generation is dependent upon time constraints.

When time is limited, the strategic thinker is often forced to compromise her investigation into the underlying causes of an issue. Understanding causation of a problem is critical to offering effective solutions. In time-sensitive situations, she is forced to rely on experience to determine the ultimate cause for the current dilemma. The value of the solution becomes dependent upon her ability to diagnose the problem quickly. Time pressure makes this process very subjective.

Time pressure also limits her ability to try out her hypothesis or theory. A top performer almost always employs an iterative decision-making process. She tests out a solution and makes adjustments and improvements to ascertain that the final answer is the most effective alternative. Severely limiting the amount of time she has to work on a problem will stifle this iterative process and will result in the need for making more changes "on the fly" once the solution is deployed.

This process plays out in real time whenever products are sold to consumers, such as in the case of a farmer's market. A vendor selling fruit must continually evaluate the demand for the fruit based upon the time left before it spoils. As the window of time decreases, the vendor reduces the price to stimulate demand. However, if the flow of traffic through his stand is strong, the vendor may decide to hold firm on his price, only reducing it if the buyers show resistance.

Having too much time can also be an issue. In situations where time is unlimited, people often try to capture too much information. Because it is almost impossible to complete truly exhaustive research on any topic, these attempts at "boiling the ocean" result in analysis paralysis.

Control

A successful individual immediately assesses how much of the situation is within his control and how much is not. Once he breaks the problem down along those lines, he can immediately formulate his plan of attack.

It's important to note that, when a critical element of a situation is out of his control, a strategic thinker always looks for ways to influence that aspect of the decision. Often, he may be able to affect it in an indirect way. It is this creativity that is the hallmark of strategic thinking.

In a perfect scenario, a strategic thinker will have control over all aspects of a situation or problem. When this happens, he often produces amazingly creative results that no one ever dreamed were possible. This is particularly true when a strategic thinker is involved in formulating plans for a future endeavor.

Unfortunately, even perfect scenarios sometimes produce fiascos. I often hear publishers lament the poor sales of a well-written book. They go on and on about how it just did not sell up to expectations in the first 90 days.

Strategic thinking is often underutilized in the book publishing industry, even though virtually every aspect of the decision-making process related to a book is within the publisher's control. The publisher controls the price at which the book sells, the dollars attached to its marketing campaign, the release date, the content of the book, and the packaging. Furthermore, the publisher controls the time period used to evaluate the success of the book's sales.

If a book were marketed like a consumer product—given a sales evaluation period of one year, given a marketing budget that represented a percentage of the per unit retail price, and packaged and released in conjunction with timely events (e.g., cookbooks during the holidays)—the results might be quite different.

Experience

Experience is a true double-edged sword for the strategic thinker. Having too much experience can limit creativity in generating alternatives. Having little or no experience will increase the time needed to solve the problem or create a plan.

Most strategic thinkers prefer to have the experience available and use it as a resource, but make a concerted effort to keep an open mind when it comes to the status quo. They realize that many problems are created due to the hidebound thought, "That's the way we've always done it."

Experience can be a great teacher. It can also be a conniving and deceitful mistress and lure you down the path of ill repute. Strategic thinkers are very careful in their use of experience. Their goal is to understand history and learn from it, not necessarily to repeat it.

Retail stores always look at past history when evaluating holiday sales. They base inventory decisions, at least partially, upon how certain products have historically sold. Their goal is to understand what did not sell well and why, so that they do not place large orders for similar items in the future.

The Unknown

At every step in the strategic-thinking process, the successful individual is asking herself the question, "What don't I know?" In the early stages of problem solving, this question is critical to formulating a research plan. In the later stages, the decision maker must reconcile which unknowns she can live with against those she can't and make a decision. In most cases, it will be impossible to explore all of the unknown factors that go into a plan or a decision. The superachiever must be comfortable with the ambiguity that remains. The best decision makers set up contingency plans for the results of ambiguous situations.

Every plan that a strategic thinker devises has a list of unknowns. In a workgroup situation, these items are often listed along with the factors that will resolve the ambiguity. Not surprisingly, other strategic-thinking factors play a large part in resolving the unknown. Having more time, more experience (or historical information), or more control often help clear the fog of the unknown. Although there will always be a set of facts that are unknown, the decision maker must make her decision and be confident that she is prepared for all the contingencies.

For example, the chef in a restaurant is never certain exactly how many people will eat dinner in her establishment each evening. Yet, she needs to be prepared for the possibility that, if no one comes, she will need to store her perishable products for another day, and that if the number of diners is double that which she expected, she will need to send someone to the store for more supplies.

Outcome Finality

Is this situation life and death—or at least career-threatening? Does it matter which decision you make? Outcome finality plays a huge role in the strategic mindset. If there is no possibility of recovery from a poor decision, the potential for emotional investment in that decision is far greater than a situation that easily lends itself to trial and error. In most cases, for example, quitting a job is a decision that has enormous finality. Even though you may be able to return to work for your former employer, you may not be able to return to that exact position.

Those top performers who exemplify Career Intensity—at all levels and in all industries—often make decisions that weigh heavily on their minds. It is almost always the finality of the outcome that creates this weight. Even if the other decision-making factors are favorable, outcome finality (or perceived outcome finality) can create enormous emotional consequences for the decision maker. Although making these decisions is often why they get paid the big bucks, compensation does not make the process any easier or any less emotional.

THE EIGHT-STEP PROCESS TO MANAGE YOUR EMOTIONS

Strategic thinking requires a cool head. Remaining calm and rational, even in the face of extreme pressure, is the hallmark of highly successful individuals. A calm veneer doesn't mean that you are unfeeling; it simply means that you are engaging the logical aspects of your thinking process. Remember that you must think like a well-run company—strategically. The following process can help you rein in your emotional response and smooth the way for successful strategic thinking:

Disassociate Yourself

If every strategic-thinking situation has an emotional aspect, then how do some people make decisions that appear to be more rational than others? People who make decisions that appear to be more rational often disassociate themselves from the project or process. This is difficult to do, but it is essential to good decision making. Surgeons, firefighters, and military commanders are forced to make decisions that have life-and-death implications—and they must do so under extreme pressure. They have mastered the ability to temporarily separate themselves from the emotion of the situation. A successful strategic thinker views a problem as though she is completely detached from the circumstances surrounding it. By viewing the situation through this lens, she is objective in her assessment of the challenge. She prevents her personal emotional investment from playing a role in the moment.

Define Specific Outcomes

Identify what this decision-making process or plan will accomplish. It is always helpful to start with the ideal outcome—even if it does not appear realistic or possible. Once you set the ideal outcome as the goal for your decision or plan, you activate the creative side of your brain. At this stage, you only want to make certain that the outcome is possible. You are not concerned with probability.

For example, when making a decision to price a product, a company must decide at what point the most units will sell for the most profit. If they price the product too low, they will not make enough money and they will run out of inventory. If they price the product too high, they will not sell enough of the product to break even. The company is seeking to drive a specific outcome—optimal profit.

Acknowledge Your Instincts

What is that gut feeling or intuition anyway? Is it something real, tangible, or merely a thought that pounds at you like a bass drum?

It is important that you acknowledge any feelings you have about the problem or the desired outcome. At the outset of your decision-making process, list possible solutions based solely on instinct. These hypotheses will free you from the nagging of your emotional subconscious. Generating purely emotional solutions upfront will put them into perspective as you complete your research.

An experienced contractor can look at the plans to a home he is building and determine where potential problems will arise from shortage of materials. In making a decision about which vendor he will choose to supply materials for construction, the contractor can use historical delivery records to determine who has the best track record.

The contractor has worked with all of the vendors before, and he knows them all well. He knows their strengths and weaknesses, and he has a "gut feeling" about each of them. He needs to acknowledge this gut feeling and weigh it against the historical delivery records of each vendor and the importance of the timing of product delivery.

Acknowledging his gut instinct first—the emotional aspect of the decision—frees the contractor up to make a rational decision about which materials supplier to use.

Research the Problem

Now you must find the root cause of the problem or the most basic critical factor in your decision or plan. The goal here is to get to the heart of the matter and address the issue once and for all time. Let's take the case of a restaurant owner who is having trouble with complaints of cold food from diners in the restaurant. The key is to trace the problem down to the root cause and find out why the food is cold when it reaches the customers' tables. There are several factors that may contribute to this problem, such as distance of the dining room from the kitchen; not using plate covers; the speed of the service; the waiting time from preparation to service; and the temperatures of the dining room and the kitchen. However, none of these contributing factors will make any difference if the food is not cooked to the proper temperature in the first place. In this example, improper cooking temperature is the root cause of the problem. Looking for the root cause is the primary purpose of your research.

In the case of strategic planning, the goal is to get to the most basic level of the desired outcome so that you can take as few steps as possible in order to achieve your goal. You are looking for the shortest distance between where you are now and where you want to go. For example, let's say you are a salesperson working on commission and your goal is to increase your salary by 20 percent by the end of the year. For planning purposes, the shortest distance to your goal is to sell more products to your customers. Therefore, researching ways to increase product sales is the best place to begin.

Recognize Patterns

After finding the root cause of your problem or the shortest distance to your goal, you should begin to work backwards toward your current state. In doing this, you will notice factors that contribute to the root cause of the problem. In planning, you will find steps that will contribute to overall goal achievement. You should look for patterns in these contributing factors. As patterns emerge, you must begin to look for ways to enable desired behavior and permanently discontinue undesirable behavior.

For example, Pete is always late for work on Fridays. When he does arrive, he is often disheveled and disorganized. He is also tired on Fridays and has even fallen asleep in his office a few times. This behavior has occurred every Friday for the past five weeks. Every other day of the week, Pete is the model employee.

Because Pete's boss recognized this pattern, she was able to approach him in a nonthreatening way by simply asking if he needed to change his schedule to work a later shift on Friday mornings.

It turned out that Pete's wife was working the night shift at the hospital on Thursday evenings and Pete was watching their eight-month-old baby on Thursday nights. A schedule shift for the next three months was the perfect solution.

Generate Alternatives

Once you have identified your goal and have conducted enough research to recognize patterns that will lead to its achievement, you should begin to look for potential actions that can help you move from your current state to your desired state. Because you're apt to react more emotionally when you are backed into a corner, give yourself options in assessing the situation.

There is a purchasing agent I know who makes a list of the three best vendors for each product he buys. He sorts this list based upon price, delivery time, and quality. He often has three different vendors for each of these categories. When he needs a specific product, he automatically has options based upon which aspect of this decision is most critical.

In some cases, having multiple alternatives is helpful, while in others, it may be detrimental. The goal is to make an exhaustive list of options, and each option must be mutually exclusive. In other words, each option on its own can potentially solve the problem.

Assess Risk

Now that you have a list of options to help you achieve your goal or solve a problem, you need to look at each of the options in front of you and evaluate each of them from a risk perspective. In doing so, you need to look at two factors: the amount of risk and the probability that negative consequences will occur.

For example, a restaurant manager needs to close his restaurant for a day to perform roof repairs. The noise and the presence of workmen on ladders in the dining room will inconvenience the guests. In order to choose which day of the week to close, the manager must assess the risk of lost business based on historical information and patterns of patronage.

Select a Solution

Your goal is to select the option that will help you achieve your goal or solve your problem while minimizing your risk. You are, in essence, selecting the best option or, depending upon the situation, the option that is least bad. In the case of the restaurant manager, he will minimize his risk by closing his restaurant on the day of the week that generates the least revenue.

This may appear to be a very involved task. Once internalized, however, it will become second nature.

PLAN FOR CONTINGENCIES

Legend has it that a chess grand master can view every move on the board before it is even played. Chess grand masters are classic strategic thinkers. Likewise, superachievers consider virtually every possible outcome from every situation before it happens. Imagine spending a day in the mind of a natural strategic thinker. Every situation is optimized to produce the maximum return on time invested. All possible scenarios have been thought through and those with viable alternatives reside in a special place in this person's mind, just waiting to be called upon, if necessary.

I once had the opportunity to work with a person who was a natural strategic thinker. He made decisions very quickly and welcomed people who asked questions about alternatives they thought he had not considered. It was truly amazing to listen to him rattle alternatives off the top of his head as though he had already lived them and met with the unfortunate consequences offered by some of the proposed solutions. The truth of the matter is that he *had* already lived every scenario—in his mind. His experience had provided him with a catalogue of references that his subconscious allowed him to access as needed. When he did not have experience in a certain area, he instantly listed out alternatives and calculated the probability of success of each option. When asked how often he was correct, he reported that it was about 80 percent of the time.

When asked to describe his thought process, he said, "In every situation, I ask myself what the possible outcomes could be. I then try to decide what the likelihood—the odds—of each outcome might be. I do this on a comparative basis and not mathematically. For example, I say 'Scenario A is more likely than scenario B, but scenario C is more likely than A, so we must prepare for C.' Once I do this, I then think of my reaction, from the most likely scenario to the least likely scenario. I am very rarely surprised."

When I asked him if any situations had arisen for which he was not prepared, he responded, "It takes a very creative individual to come up with an alternative that I have not anticipated. I was recently surprised by a colleague's departure to a competing firm. The gentleman had 20 years of experience with us, and yet, he went to a competitor to start up a new division. I did not see that coming."

He continued, "The gentleman in question was asked to retire by our boss. I did not know that. Although he was at retirement age, he still had a significant amount of value to contribute to the organization. He was pushed out by our boss, who wanted a man he had previously worked with in that role. My friend was not ready to retire. If I had known what our boss was thinking, I would probably have seen that situation coming."

Anticipating all the alternatives in any situation is never easy. Most people don't even try. It is simply easier to choose a solution based upon gut instinct and then hope for the best. However, the most successful people in business—those with Career Intensity—look at all the possible alternatives to each and every situation. They have on some level conducted an analysis of the probability of each scenario actually happening and have several solutions mentally prepared in case they need them.

There is a system that you can employ to help you develop personal contingency plans: thinking in extremes. The theory behind this system is that if you are mentally prepared for the most extreme scenario, you can easily adjust your plan to something less extreme. As you think about your long-term career strategy, ask yourself questions, such as, "What would I do if someone offered me a job that paid me twice as much money but required me to travel 25 percent more?" Generate several alternatives that you can think through. It's fine if you don't come up with an answer right away. The thought process is what is important. Also ask yourself, "What would I do if I lost my job tomorrow?" Although this is not a pleasant thought, it is the other extreme and needs to be considered as part of your personal contingency planning process.

Play this game with yourself whenever you have the opportunity. As you master the art of thinking in extremes, you will be far ahead of your competition and you will be prepared for whatever life throws at you. Look at the extremes for each scenario you find yourself in during the day. After a while, you will be able to internalize this behavior and it will become automatic. When that happens, you will notice a boost of self-confidence because you will have thought through virtually any situation that may arise.

Once you have mentally prepared yourself for the possible alternatives in each situation, you should make certain you are prepared for the pressure that will accompany the need to use them. Your mind cannot differentiate between what is real and what is imagined. You should imagine yourself in circumstances that require you to implement one of your extreme contingency plans. Add the element of time pressure to the situation. As children, we did this countless times. I can remember standing on the foul line of a basketball court, pretending that the fate of the game was resting on me making the very next shot. You should do the exact same thing with your contingency plans. Make the situation as realistic and as dramatic as possible. Drill yourself on each plan over and over until you can work it from memory.

CREATIVITY AND STRATEGIC THINKING

Strategy and creativity are inseparable. As a strategic thinker, you must be able to come up with solutions that other people can't see or may have overlooked. There are ways to stimulate your strategic creativity that many people take for granted. Although you will need to explore alternatives that get your creative juices flowing, top performers have reported that they use the following methods to stimulate their personal strategic creativity:

Find a Stress Release

A major byproduct of stress is increased fatigue. Be certain to get sufficient rest and drink plenty of fluids during times of high stress. Find a form of stress release that will allow you to decompress after periods of focused concentration. Many people turn to exercise or meditation, which are natural and helpful to both your body and your mind.

If you have just completed a large strategic project and you have accomplished everything you set out to achieve, reward yourself with a day off. In fact, someone who thinks deeply in planning or problem solving should spend as much time away from their task as they spend working at it. For instance, if your job requires that you concentrate deeply for four consecutive hours, then you should spend at least four hours away from that task immediately following the four-hour session. The reasoning behind this is straightforward. Your mind needs time to absorb and synthesize the information. Four consecutive hours is the maximum period of peak mental productivity you should expect from yourself. After that four-hour period, take a break and focus on something else. You will be surprised how different the situation appears when you come back to it.

Embrace Boredom

Boredom is good for thinking creatively. Great artists often go years between creating works of art. Imagine if an artist walked into a studio and tried to force a masterpiece. It would not work. You should view boredom or restlessness as the calm before the creative storm. Allow your mind to wander and welcome the quiet time that precedes the creative process.

Take Time-Out

If you are working on a project that requires focused concentration and energy, arrange for someone else to help you with your normal activities. If you feel particularly focused at 2:00 a.m., you must respect the momentum you have and finish your thought process. Suppressing your creative energy will make it that much more difficult the next time you are inspired. In those rare bursts of creativity that are all-consuming, rely on someone to cover for you on your other tasks. Make arrangements to do so in advance.

Walk Around

Some people find that ideas flow much more freely when they are walking or running. Others report that ideas come to them while they are in the shower. It seems that activity, particularly a routine activity that does not require a great deal of concentration, often frees up the mind to wander creatively.

I am particularly inspired by long walks. I carry a pen and a pad of paper with me everywhere. As I walk, I write down the ideas that pop into my head. I don't spend time trying to focus my thoughts. I let them flow naturally. It is amazing how many great ideas were born as I walked along the streets of New York City.

Tap into Your Subconscious

As previously discussed, many of your thoughts, feelings, and desires are present in your subconscious. In essence, you are thinking about your decisions or the plans you are making even when you are not actively focused on them. If you have ever had the solution to a problem just come to you, it was the result of your processing the problem on a subconscious level. Top performers confirm that the more focused or intense their strategic thinking is on a conscious level, the more their subconscious mind can help them solve problems. The order and structure of the process discussed in this chapter will help your subconscious mind sort through options based upon your experience.

There are two ways to help facilitate this subconscious mental processing. The first is to write down everything associated with the issue at hand. There does not need to be any order to the information at this stage. Just get it all down on paper or in your computer. Carry the documents around with you for a few days and reflect upon them when you have spare moments. These reflections don't need to be long and involved. Just read through your list a couple of times. I do this on the subway or bus, while waiting for a meeting to start, or in the office while on hold on the phone. Next, organize the thoughts into some type of outline. Again, format is secondary to actually handling the information and processing it mentally. You may notice that some new ideas have come to you and they fit into the information that you have already written down. You may also notice patterns start to emerge or that you have new areas to explore. Then, write the situation out in narrative form, as though you were writing a story based upon the outline you constructed. After you do that, leave it alone for a while. If you have the time, a couple of days works best. During this period, try not to think about the situation at all. Actively put it out of your mind. After a few days have passed and you revisit the situation, you will be astonished at how different it looks and how much easier the information will flow. You will be able to concentrate on this issue or plan until it is complete. If you're working on large or complex issues, you may need several breaks such as the one described.

The second way to help facilitate subconscious mental processing is visual. Draw pictures, maps, and diagrams of the situation or plan. Draw many different types of charts and sketches. The accuracy or aesthetic value of the drawing is unimportant; you are trying to activate your thought process. Post these charts or pictures where you can see them regularly. I hang mine in my home, in my office, and in conspicuous places where I can see them while thinking about other things. (The back of the bathroom door is great for this purpose.) Next, arrange the drawings like a storyboard. Place several of the drawings on a wall next to one another as though you were trying to find a way to make them into a movie. Then, remove yourself from the situation for a few days. Take the storyboard out of the room and put it in a closet. When you bring it back out in a day or two, you will be amazed with the new perspective you have on your issue or plan. Your subconscious mind will have been working on completing your movie in vivid detail.

Chapter Four

ATTACK YOUR GOALS

Goals are essential to the process of continuous improvement. Without goals, you are a rudderless ship at the mercy of the current—drifting from one place to the next. Setting proper goals is almost as important as having goals in the first place. Your goals should be realistic and coincide with your value system. If you are four feet tall, for example, winning the Most Valuable Player award in the NBA next year is not a realistic goal for you. Likewise, if you're an atheist, your goal to become a well-known pastor and have the largest congregation in the world doesn't line up with your values. If your goals are not based on who you are, what you believe, and the values you live by, you will achieve undesirable results.

Successful individuals take control of their careers by prioritizing the outcomes they desire and building goals around them. They then find ways to make those goals actionable. The accumulation of these actions over time builds into the achievement of their long-term objectives.

People with Career Intensity distinguish themselves from the rest of the world by the way they view success. A superachiever does not allow society to determine her worth. Instead, she views success through her own lens—and a unique and specific lens at that. In essence, she sets goals for herself and does not claim victory until she has achieved them. Hers is an all-or-nothing process: either she has reached her goals, or she has not. If she has not yet arrived at the point where she has reached her goal, she simply presses forward. On the surface, this process may appear very simplistic. In reality, it is one of the cornerstones to success. Only you can define your goals. When you do, you should stop at nothing to achieve your dreams.

THE POWER OF INTENTION

Freddie is a great example of someone who set his goals early, overcame his fears, and recognized opportunity when it presented itself. A successful business owner, Freddie was born in Peru and moved to the United States when he was in his early teens. He attended public high schools in New York City, and he embraced the goal of becoming an Entrepreneur from an early age. Freddie's goal was to own his own business by the time he was 25 years old.

After graduating high school, Freddie took a job with a company that cleaned office buildings. His warm personality and attention to detail help him advance rapidly in the organization. In his third year with that company, Freddie was supervising over 150 people and he was actively bringing in new business for his boss.

In his fourth year with the company, Freddie approached his boss with a business opportunity. The local office of a major corporation was seeking bids for cleaning their office space in northern New Jersey. Although Freddie encouraged his boss to bid on the project, the owner of the company did not think that expanding to northern New Jersey was a wise move. Freddie took a chance and submitted a bid on his own behalf. As it turned out, his bid was accepted, and Freddie built a company around servicing this one account. He was a business owner at 21, meeting his goal four years early.

When I asked Freddie how he felt about submitting that bid, he responded, "I was scared to death. I was more scared that they would pick me than I was that they would not pick me. But I knew that, in order to achieve my goal of owning my own business by the time I was 25, I had to begin looking for ways to go out on my own. I knew there would never be an ideal time to leave the steady income of my current job. I knew that I had to force myself to press forward and take some big steps to make my goal become a reality. At the time, I thought that submitting that bid would simply be good practice for the future. Ultimately, it was one of the defining moments of my life."

You may be thinking that Freddie just got lucky, or that he was in the right place at the right time. In reality, Freddie's situation demonstrates how an individual with a goal-oriented mindset can use his own definition of success to help him make his business dreams a reality. This mindset is also effective for people who work in a corporate environment. Defining your own success is critically important, no matter what your life ambitions may be.

My personal experience is that, when I graduated from college at the age of 20, I wanted to work in the hospitality industry. I knew that, because the entry-level salaries in this industry were not generous, I could only afford to work in an area where the rent was reasonable. During the last few months of my senior year in college, I commuted from Providence, Rhode Island, where I was attending Johnson & Wales University, to Tarrytown, New York, on the weekends. I did this so that I could work at the Westchester Marriott. My goal was to enter the management development program in the Westchester County area upon graduation. If I was successful, I could live with my parents while I was in training—a significant financial advantage at the beginning of my career.

The commute was a tough one. In order to achieve my goal of getting into the management development program, I had to be a full-time employee for six months. These training positions were highly coveted, and there were several other candidates vying for this particular position at the Westchester Marriott. My last class of the week was dismissed at 1:00 p.m. on Thursday and my first class was early Monday morning. Every weekend, from Thursday evening through Sunday evening, I clocked in 40 hours at the Marriott.

I graduated from college seven months after I started working at the Westchester Marriott and I was accepted into the management development program two weeks after graduation. During my interview with members of Marriott's Management Candidacy Review Board, I outlined how I had a very specific career path planned. I had goals for specific positions I wanted to be in by certain dates. My career plan included becoming a hotel general manager by the time I was 35 years old. Although most of the board members thought this was aggressive, a few of them let me know that having a plan, and having specific measurement criteria for my own personal success, was a determining factor in offering me the management development position. Incidentally, I achieved my ultimate goal five years early—I became a general manager at the age of 30.

The sense of personal accomplishment from achieving a goal (or goals) that you have personally developed creates confidence. This confidence leads to even greater achievement in all aspects of life. You should view goal setting just as you would view planning a long trip. Before you set out on your journey, you look at a map to make sure you understand where you need to go. On that map there may be several different routes that will lead you to your destination. Before you leave your home and get on the road, you check each of the various routes and select the one that you believe will get you to your destination in the fastest and most direct fashion. You may change course several times during your journey, but the knowledge that you will arrive at your destination is never in doubt. You know that you have a good plan to get there within a specific time frame. This is exactly how you should view the goal-setting process—as a process of building a roadmap for success. The knowledge that you will reach your destination should never be in doubt.

JUDGING YOUR OWN SUCCESS

A critical lesson to be learned here is that you should be the only judge of your own success. Only you know what the roadmap to your destination looks like. Pretend that you are going on a long journey with some friends. You all start out from the same location. Everyone knows that it will take several days to get to the place you want to go. Everyone knows where that place is, but the friends you are traveling with do not know how to get there. You are the only person who has the map that will help you find your destination. Only you know which landmarks along the way will help keep you on course. How do you think the other travelers feel? Do you think they have blind faith that you will reach your destination? Some of them may, but the majority probably has doubts. They may believe that you have selected a destination that is too far from home or that may require too difficult a journey. They may also feel that you don't know how to get from point A to point B. You have the map and only you can judge whether or not you are on course.

Time and again I have seen people set standards for others that were far too low, and they ended up shortchanging the potential of the individual. Only you know how much talent, skill, and knowledge you bring to any task that you attempt. Others have no true way of assessing your potential. In addition, only you can gauge your motivation toward achievement. Because no one has access to those aspects of your personality, they can't judge whether or not you are capable of achieving your goals.

If you allow others to define your successes, they will ultimately define your future. It is crucial that you look at your future through your own lens and that you assess your own effort toward success. It is the only way to control your destiny.

PURSUING YOUR OBSESSION

Most successful people describe the pursuit of their goals as an obsession. When I speak to them, they state clearly that their careers began to change course when they focused solely on the achievement of their goals—often to the detriment of other aspects of their lives.

I am not advocating that you take an unhealthy approach toward goal achievement. I'm not telling you to avoid your family and friends and only concentrate on the goals you have outlined for yourself. What I am saying is that, in order to achieve your goals and make your dreams come true, you need to spend as much time as possible working toward them.

You may ask yourself how you can align your daily activities with the goals you have set for yourself. This question is particularly perplexing because you're working with a time frame that is in the distant future. Time and distance can often distort your perception of reality. In other words, because a goal is set far out into the future, you may have a difficult time believing that it is relevant to what you are doing today.

I often compare this perception of goals to the feeling of traveling in an airplane. When you are at 20,000 feet and you look out of the window of an airplane, you see the buildings of a city. Those buildings appear very small and look like tiny little toys. Your brain has a difficult time comprehending the fact that those buildings are actually several hundred feet tall and may contain thousands of people. As the plane descends and you move closer and closer to the ground, you begin to grasp the size of those buildings. You also begin to realize the magnitude of what has just happened. You have, in fact, just traveled a significant distance in a short time at an altitude that would make a bird nervous. Your mind has a difficult time comprehending concepts that are not local and in perspective.

When talking about their goals, part of the obsession top performers describe is the need to take a single step—no matter how small—each day toward achieving their dreams. Each day, these unique individuals perform at least one action that gives them perspective and moves them closer to their ultimate goals.

Another characteristic of superachievers is the competitive drive they have toward goal achievement. Although most of these individuals are externally competitive—meaning they love to compete with other people—there are those who are internally competitive—meaning they love to set and achieve goals. They live to accomplish tasks better, faster, and more efficiently than the next person, or to best their own previous performance. They love to break their own records.

Although some people are naturally competitive about every aspect of their lives, everyone feels passionately about something. People with Career Intensity find a way to channel this passion toward the achievement of their goals. This passion stokes the fire that fuels that internal competitive drive. They tend this fire and cultivate it so that it burns continuously. Intrepreneurs and Entrepreneurs find new and exciting ways to challenge themselves and keep up the motivation necessary to make their goals a reality.

In most cases, this passion occurs naturally. The goals that these top achievers select are born from that passion. The people who are superstars are the ones who enjoy the process of achieving the goal as much as they enjoy the reward that is associated with the goal itself. For these individuals, the process of goal setting is truly as much about the journey as it is the destination.

THE 3-9-27 PYRAMID

The goals of top achievers have a number of characteristics in common. The first element is the number of goals. The fewer the number of goals, the greater the focus dedicated to achieving each of the individual objectives. Fewer goals equals more direct focus and, often, greater speed to completion. In fact, some of the most successful people I have met over the years have a single purpose to their entire lives. They spend every waking moment obsessed with achieving their primary goals. Although these individuals are few and far between, and this type of lifestyle can have negative consequences if not managed appropriately, their obsession does help us understand the power of goal setting.

The most effective paradigm for the goal-setting process is a three-tiered methodology that I call the 3-9-27 Pyramid. The first tier consists of long-term goals. The time frame for these goals should be no longer than ten years out. According to most top achievers I've talked to, the ten-year window is long enough to help you shape your vision of the future, but short enough to be within reach. When goals extended beyond that point into the future, most people said that their minds had more difficulty grasping the possibilities of actually achieving the goals.

The next tier of goals is medium-term, meaning that they should be achievable within one year. Each of the goals at this level should contribute toward one of the goals on the top tier. You should have no more than three sub-goals for each long-term goal. If you have three long-term goals, this gives you a total of nine goals in the middle tier.

The final tier is comprised of weekly, short-term goals. There should be no more than three supporting goals for each of the nine medium-term goals that you set. The idea is to make certain that you are taking action as frequently as possible to achieve your overall plan for the long term. Every weekly goal contributes to completion of a medium-term goal, which, in turn, supports the achievement of a long-term goal. This will give you a maximum total of 27 short-term goals each week.

To make this easier to understand, I have changed the terminology to specifically reflect what each tier represents. The long-term goals, set to be achieved within a maximum time period of ten years or less, are called Overarching Goals. The medium-term goals, which are benchmarked for completion in a one-year time frame, are Contributory Goals (because their accomplishment will contribute to the achievement of the Overarching Goal). The weekly goals are Action Items because they are very specific tasks that you can complete each day.

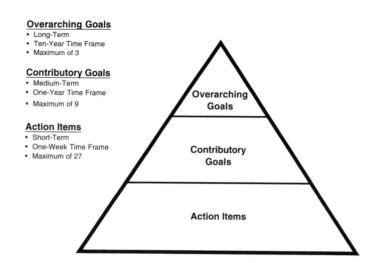

Overarching Goals
• Long-Term
• Ten-Year Time Frame
• Maximum of 3

Contributory Goals
• Medium-Term
• One-Year Time Frame
• Maximum of 9

Action Items
• Short-Term
• One-Week Time Frame
• Maximum of 27

Overarching Goals

Contributory Goals

Action Items

The general principle behind this approach toward goal setting is to make certain that you are taking frequent action that will lead toward the completion of your long-term goals.

There are numerous benefits of this goal-setting philosophy. I often find that people achieve their Overarching Goals faster then they had originally anticipated. One of the reasons for this is that the action they take on a regular basis drives their behavior. Many people report that they waste less time when they have specific action items that must be accomplished each week. Additionally, many people find that they develop a laser-like focus on each and every task they tackle. This occurs because they feel that they must spend their valuable time in accomplishing tasks that will lead toward their ultimate goals.

DEVELOPING GOALS FOR MAXIMUM EFFECTIVENESS

Much has been written about goal development. If you look on the Internet, there are numerous Web sites dedicated to the development and implementation of goals. Having too much information can be as problematic as not having enough information. In focusing on developing goals that will help lead to success, you must adhere to the principle that less is more. In keeping with that guideline, I will outline the very basics in effective goal development. Use these basics as a framework for developing your own goals. Feel free to adapt and adjust your goals as you see fit. They must work for you, so your opinion is the one that matters the most.

There are two guidelines that you must follow in order to make goal setting a powerful tool in your overall pursuit of success. First, the power of a goal comes in writing it down on a sheet of paper and then in reading it every day. The more frequently you read it, or even better, the more frequently you write it, the closer it comes to resembling reality. The power of the commitment that is required to transfer thoughts into action cannot be underestimated. By writing your goals down on paper, they become clear and focused. As you continually read them and write them, you begin to familiarize your brain with the possibility that these goals can become reality. If you write down your goals daily and envision the achievement of those goals in vivid detail, you will begin to convince yourself that these goals are, indeed, possible.

The second guideline in making goal setting a powerful achievement tool is to always state your goal using positive terminology. Focus on what you are going to do right rather than what is wrong with your current situation. The time for developing goals is not the time for problem diagnosis. Rather, it is the time to picture this achievement in its ideal and unadulterated state. The reading or writing of a goal should fill you with positive energy that you can focus toward a positive outcome. If the nature of your goal is to stop something from happening (or to stop doing something), you should focus on the positive consequences of that action as you write your goals.

A great example of positive goal setting is a remedy for one of the true irritants in business today—tardiness. When people arrive late for a meeting, appointment, or conversation, it communicates that they don't have respect for their own time or for the time of others. True, unforeseen circumstances sometimes cause people to be late, but those incidents are few and far between. Leaving earlier will help make up for a lot of those "unforeseen issues."

Let's say that being late has become a habit for you. You need to set a goal to never be late again. If you phrase it in just that way—"I will never be late"—your brain will perceive the message as "I will be late, never." This will reinforce the unacceptable behavior of arriving after the meeting has already started.

A better way to phrase that goal would be, "I will always be on time for all business meetings." This positive goal will help program your subconscious mind to reinforce your need and desire to be on time for each meeting.

Setting SMART Goals

I have always been a proponent of setting goals based upon the SMART goal development methodology. Many individuals have taken credit for the development of this acronym over the years, and although I would love to give credit where credit is due, it is impossible to determine who first developed this paradigm. What I do know is that it is helpful in developing effective goals at any level.

SMART stands for **S**pecific, **M**easurable, **A**chievable, **R**ealistic, and **T**angible. A goal must fit all of those criteria in order for it to make your list.

The first quality of a goal is that it is *specific*. The more detail you can bring to your goal, the more likely it is that your brain will perceive it as real. A great test to measure the specificity of your goal is in answering the five "Ws." The five Ws involved in goal setting are:

- **Who:** Who is involved? Can you accomplish this goal by yourself, or do you need the help of others?
- **What:** What specifically do you want to accomplish?
- **Where:** Is this goal specific to a location? Where will you be when you achieve this goal?
- **When:** When will you achieve this goal? It is critical that you establish a time frame for achieving each of your goals.
- **Why:** Why is achieving this goal important? List the specific benefits of accomplishing the goal.

The second quality of a goal is to make certain you can measure progress on your way toward goal accomplishment. You know that your goal is *measurable* when you can apply specific objective criteria to help track your progress toward completion. The best question to use to test the measurability of your goals is, "How will I know that I have accomplished this goal?"

Measurement has a very powerful effect on progress. Simply put, things that get measured get done. To define how you will measure your goal, ask yourself questions that begin with, How much? How many? And, How often? Use strategies such as target dates to make sure you remain on track.

The third quality your goal must have is that it must be *achievable*. In other words, it must be possible. Initially, achieving your goal may seem like a stretch. That's fine; you want a goal that will make you reach. When you set a goal that channels your passion, your brain goes to work figuring out ways to make it happen. You develop the attitudes, skills, and knowledge that help you move down the path toward achievement. Gradually, you begin to see opportunities that you may have previously missed. As you begin to take advantage of these opportunities, you bring yourself closer to the achievement of your goal.

You can attain virtually any goal you set when you plan your steps wisely and establish a time frame that allows you to carry out those steps. A goal that initially appeared distant and unattainable gradually becomes closer and more possible, not because your goal changed, but because you grew and expanded to match it. The change occurs within you. When you write out your goal, you commit to it. This builds your self-image. You begin to see yourself differently. The work you do toward goal achievement helps you believe that you are worthy of the goal. When you realize that you deserve this success, you begin to develop the traits that will help lead you toward achievement. That's the power of goal setting and achievement and why you must set goals that are achievable.

The fourth item to consider is that your goal must be *realistic*. To be realistic, a goal must represent an objective you are both willing and able to spend time and energy achieving. A goal can be challenging and still be realistic; you are the only one who can decide just how high your goal should be. You will stretch your goals as your self-confidence increases. It is critical to make sure that every goal represents substantial progress. A high goal is frequently easier to reach than a less challenging one because a minor goal requires a low level of personal motivation. Some of the hardest things you ever accomplish actually seem easy because you approach them with passion and zeal.

Finally, your goal must be *tangible*. A goal is tangible when you can experience it with at least one of the five senses. Can you taste, touch, smell, see, or hear the results? If so, then you have a tangible goal. If your goal is tangible, or when you tie a tangible goal to an intangible objective, you can envision it before it is achieved. This helps program your mind and reinforces the belief that achievement is possible.

BOAST Your Goals into Action

Goal setting is difficult. Like most things in life, goals look great on paper, but transforming them from a well-designed plan into results takes significant effort. Top performers break goal achievement down into smaller parts. They take small steps forward each day.

This is where you channel your competitive drive and obsession for success into daily action that will help you work up through your weekly action items. Remember, setting weekly action items helps you take steps each day toward achieving your medium- and long-term goals. In order to help you put your goals into action, I have condensed the five most effective strategies that superachievers use to implement their goals.

You should BOAST about your goals. I do not mean that you should brag about the fantastic goals you have created for yourself. That's not it. **BOAST** stands for **B**old, **O**pen, **A**chievement, **S**ignificant, and **T**ransformation. By examining each of these characteristics of goal implementation and the different ways you can incorporate them into attacking your weekly action items, you'll develop your plan of action.

Bold

Have you ever said to yourself, "Wow. That person really has guts"? When I was in high school, a guy I'll call Clark also attended who was two years younger than I. He was the shortest person in his class and unusually thin. Looking back, he was probably underdeveloped for his age. Clark tried out for the football team and didn't make it (mostly due to his size, not his ability). He also ran track in the spring and wrestled during the winter sports season. In my high school, these sports were not very glamorous. The glamour sports were football, basketball, and baseball. In any case, Clark was friendly with the most popular kids in his grade. He was always included in the inner circle conversations with his peer group. Most of the other popular kids in his class were jocks that played the glamour sports.

When I was a senior in high school, I had the opportunity to become friendly with a sophomore. One day, I asked his opinion about the secret to Clark's success. He responded, "Clark is fearless. He does not know—or does not care—about his size. He will do whatever it takes to get what he wants. Every girl in the tenth grade loves him, but he has his sights aimed higher. He only wants to surround himself with the best—and he's told everyone that he wants to date only the prettiest and most successful girl in school. I bet he makes that happen."

Sure enough, he did. In May of my senior year in high school, Clark showed up at the senior prom, as a sophomore, with a beautiful three-sport athlete who was all-county in girls' basketball, soccer, and field hockey.

The lesson here is simple to understand, but difficult to put into practice. When you have identified a goal, you should take bold action to bring it to fruition. The meek may inherit the earth in a spiritual sense, but in the pursuit of your goals, you must take bold action. Remember, only you can be the judge of your success or failure. If you act boldly and you do not achieve your objective, ignore the laughter or commentary of others. Press onward with even more bold action.

Open

Open communication of your goals may be a tough one for you to swallow. Some of my friends who work for Coca-Cola USA provided me with a great example of the value of open communication. Coke has an aggressive sales culture. One of the things that contributes to the company's success in this area is something they call "track, rank, and publish," a methodology that is fairly common in sales organizations. Here is how it works: At the beginning of the year, each salesperson sits down with her manager and commits to achieving a goal (usually a quantity goal based on cases of soda). They break her goals down into weekly sales targets. Each week, the organization tracks the performance of the sales representative and publishes the percentage of cases sold compared to her goal in a newsletter, on their intranet, and on bulletin boards throughout their facilities all over the country. This open communication of goals and publication of progress stimulates the competitive drive in each of the sales representatives. Many have told me that the publication of results in this way is more of a motivating factor than the threat of disciplinary action from their bosses.

You may be asking yourself, "How can I use this technique to help me in the achievement of my goals?" One way is to choose someone with whom you share a mutual trust and respect—a spouse or a friend usually works well. Sit down with him and explain to him that you have some very important goals that you want to achieve in your life and that you need someone to dialogue with on a weekly basis. Explain to your friend that you are not looking for someone to pass judgment on your goals, but rather are seeking someone with whom you can share your progress. This individual absolutely cannot sit in judgment of what you are trying to accomplish. He must listen, offer words of encouragement, and celebrate your success. You should meet with him weekly, either in person or over the phone. Share your goals and your feedback on the progress you have made during the course of the week. He should spend 90 percent of this meeting listening and 10 percent of the meeting offering you encouragement that will help you stick with your plan.

Achievement

The next step in the implementation plan is adopting an attitude of daily achievement. This simply means that you must do something every day, no matter how small, that moves you closer toward achieving your goals. You do not have to complete an entire action item; rather, you must take incremental action toward the completion of a goal.

As an example, let's say that you have a major project due at work at the end of the month. This is one of those projects that hangs over your head like a fog over an open field. This project is clouding the view of everything else you have to get done—and your boss just gave you an urgent task that will require your full attention for the next three days.

The challenge is to maintain some sense of momentum and progress on the really important project that is due at the end of the month while completing the urgent assignment that your boss just dropped in your lap.

This is where achievement comes in. When you break your goals into smaller tasks, you can complete a little piece each day and maintain your sense of momentum and progress. In the case of the major project, at lunch you can set up a checklist to help you organize the project, and on your way home, you fill in the items on the checklist. The next day, you spend fifteen minutes prioritizing the items while you drink your coffee. Each day you must do something that moves you closer to your goal. This is the approach I took to writing this book. Each day, I spent a dedicated amount of time working on it. Some days it was just a few minutes, and other days it was hours, but each day I did something. I kept the momentum going, and eventually, I was amazed to discover that my daily writing efforts had produced a significant amount of information.

Significant

Your goals are important. In fact, they need to be the most significant aspect of your work life. They must become your priority because your goals are shaping your future. If you want to take control of your business life and you've developed three long-term business goals, then you need to make darn sure that you elevate these goals to a position of significance in your career.

I'm often asked to quantify how much time should be focused on goal achievement. My answer usually startles most people. The most successful people I work with are always working toward goal achievement—100 percent of the time. Either they are actively working on a task that will move them closer to achieving their goals, or they are using an accelerant to help them go forward. When it comes to work, top performers put their entire effort toward achieving their goals. In order to transform your dreams into reality, your current job and your career ambitions must be aligned. If you are in a job where there is limited benefit to your ongoing development as well as the development of the company, you should carefully consider alternatives to your employment situation.

People often report that many of their job requirements do not help them advance in their careers. They raise issues such as monotonous reports they need to complete or time-consuming meetings they need to attend. I agree that some tasks can be counterproductive and often big wastes of time, but they also provide an opportunity for creativity. Look for ways to make the processes more efficient and make these mundane requirements obsolete. In some cases, you might be able to make a case to your boss to eliminate the unproductive activity. In other instances, you may be able to train someone else to handle that aspect of your work in return for completing one of their assignments that will be more beneficial to you. You need to be creative in aligning your goals with your current job responsibilities.

The significance of a goal is not about obsession. Rather, the significance relates to which items become goals. Something that is simply nice to have should not be a goal. That is more of a whim or a desire. You know that your goal is significant when there are dire consequences for its lack of achievement. Understanding the consequences is one of the keys to staying motivated.

I work with an outstanding company whose budgeting process provides a perfect example of tying goals to consequences. At this company, each regional manager is allowed to set her own budgeted profit number. At the end of the year, the managers' collective budgeted profit numbers must equal the targeted profit growth for the company. No regional manager is allowed to budget for stagnant or negative growth and those with more resources are required to grow proportionately.

The minimum standards for the regional managers are positive growth. If a region does not grow over the course of a year, that regional manager is put on probation. If the regional manager does not show profit growth during the six months after she goes on probation, she is fired.

The goal of growing the business is significant to that regional manager because there are consequences associated with not achieving it. Everything she does at work is tied into that goal in some way.

In your career, there must be significant consequences associated with not achieving your goals. They must be real to you. Let's say you want to start your own business but you can't seem to focus on that goal. The consequence of not achieving that goal is that you will have to work for your boss (who is a jerk) for a longer period of time. Depending upon how much you hate your boss, the significance of this goal may be enough to keep you motivated during the most difficult tasks associated with starting your own business.

Transformation

Significance and transformation go hand in hand. Once you elevate your goals to a position of significance, you must begin to transform your life to the point where you spend as much time and energy possible in the pursuit of your goals. Although it may not be realistic to devote 100 percent of your time toward achieving your goals, the closer you can get to 100 percent, the faster you will accomplish the great things you have planned for yourself.

I am working with a single mother of two young girls who is very ambitious in her career. Even though she has fantastic career ambitions, only one of her three Overarching Goals is work-related. She has another goal related to the development of her girls and a third goal concerning her health and fitness. How much time do you think she spends working toward achieving one of these three goals? In a difficult week, she spends somewhere north of 90 percent of her time working toward achieving each one of these Overarching Goals. This woman has realistically assessed her life and has created three goals that she feels are of utmost significance to her and her family. She has transformed her whole life into a focus on achieving those goals. When situations arise each week that are not be directly related to the pursuit of her goals, she handles them as efficiently as she can while keeping her goals in constant perspective.

IDENTIFYING AND USING ACCELERANTS

An accelerant is a tool that will help you progress more quickly toward the achievement of your goals. There are four major accelerants that can help expedite your progress toward goal achievement: people, technology, experience, and time.

People

Those individuals who succeed on a consistent basis are able to accomplish many things at one time. They do not, however, tackle all tasks by themselves. Top performers often have other people help them. In fact, these folks have other people line up to help them achieve their goals. They do it by creating a win-win scenario for the individual who is the accelerant. A great example of this strategy is a mentor-protégée relationship. The protégée benefits from the learning associated with completing tasks that are critical to the mentor, and the mentor offers guidance on how the protégée can achieve greater success in life. In many organizations, there are internship positions where tasks that are often tedious and time-consuming are tackled by people who embrace the opportunity to learn about a business from the ground up. I know many superachievers who began their careers in this fashion—by assuming unpaid or low-paying internship positions.

Another way people can function as an accelerant in goal achievement is by combining like responsibilities. For example, if you and a friend both have the desire to refinance your homes, one of you can interview mortgage brokers while the other can research property values in the local area. In this way, you each can focus deeply in your area of responsibility and generate the best quality solution for each option.

There are literally hundreds of ways that people can serve as accelerants dedicated toward goal achievement. The critical element of this strategy is to make sure the other person is getting something out of helping you achieve your goal.

Technology

Technology is another widely available accelerant. In particular, the area of communication has benefited directly from technological accelerants. You can now e-mail, fax, or leave a voicemail for anyone at any hour of the day or night. This asynchronous communication is effective when you have task-oriented items to cover with friends or colleagues.

Interactive or synchronous communication has also benefited from evolving technologies. Mobile phones, two-way messaging devices, and instant messaging all offer you the opportunity to communicate anywhere at any time. This has taken multitasking to a new level. A word of caution in your use of technology as an accelerant: Be certain that the technology serves your purpose. It should be a means to an end and not an end unto itself. I know many a gadget-guy who has become paralyzed by his use of technology.

Experience

It has often been said that history is a great teacher. In the realm of individual achievement, history falls under the umbrella of experience. You may recall that Chapter Three discussed the value of experience in planning and decision making. Experience also plays a valuable role in the tactical aspect of goal achievement. There are two different ways experience can help facilitate goal achievement.

The first way experience can hasten the achievement of your goals is when you have direct experience in the same or a similar situation. If you have direct, relevant experience, you can rely on it as a rough roadmap to guide you through the completion of the task at hand. If your previous experience was not successful, you know at a minimum some of the potential pitfalls you may face in the completion of the task. If your previous experience was successful, you can recall the past experience and look at ways to improve your efficiency in this next attempt.

A second way experience can serve as an accelerant is when the relevant experience is available to you in the form of another person's success. The beauty of this method is that you don't need to have an actual relationship with the person to use their success to your advantage. For example, you are using my experience as an accelerant right now. To use the success of another person as an accelerant for your own goal achievement, you need only to have access to a recorded history of their success methodology. You can then replicate their behavior and duplicate their success. There is no need to reinvent the wheel.

Time

You can also use time as an accelerant. Put another way, if you don't use time to your advantage, it will most certainly work against you as a disadvantage. Time is one of the aspects in life that is black and white. It either helps you, or it hurts you. It is never neutral.

A great example of using time as an accelerant is in a negotiation process. If one party has to make a decision by a certain date, time is certainly not in that party's favor. Time is, however, a huge advantage to the party who is making the offer—provided they know about the time pressure faced by the other side.

Another example of time as an accelerant is the principal of compounding interest. If you placed $1,000 per year in a tax-exempt, interest-bearing account in 1950 and you earned the average rate of return of 11 percent, you would have had $1.85 million in your account by the year 2000. In this case, time acted as an accelerant. If you were unable to save any money at all prior to the time you turned 55, you would have a difficult task ahead of you in trying to save enough money for your retirement at age 65. Time would be working against you.

People, technology, experience, and time are the four most common accelerants leveraged by successful people as they focus on goal achievement. There are certainly others. Your only limit in finding accelerants to help you achieve your goals is your creativity or, better yet, the creativity of those around you.

PREPARING FOR LIMITLESS POSSIBILITIES

There is a question you need to ask yourself each day as you review your goals. This question is central to your ability to make your ambitions become reality. That question is, "What are you prepared to do?" Essentially, what are you prepared to sacrifice to make your goals become reality? The sacrifice may be temporary, or it may be permanent. It may be long-term, or it may be short-term. It may involve finance, or it may involve quality of life. You should ask yourself this question repeatedly. Ask it during your goal development and during your implementation planning. Ask it each day as you review your goals and evaluate your progress.

You have made it through every challenge you've ever faced. And you have what it takes to get through many, many more. It can be frightening to stretch yourself and test your strength. It can also be energizing and invigorating. Go after your goals. Be aggressive and never quit. Don't let difficult situations keep you from moving forward, ever closer to your goals.

Overcoming a difficult challenge can bring you a level of satisfaction that you cannot reach in any other way. Along with that satisfaction comes a solid confidence of knowing for certain that you've done it before, and you can do it again.

When you seek challenge, you end up gaining achievement. By welcoming each challenge, you're expressing and expanding your own confidence in a way that is truly genuine and enduring.

There was a time when you were challenged by many of the things you can now do without a second thought. Think of how far you've come as a result of your willingness to take on those challenges. And think of how very far you still can go when you welcome each challenge as the great opportunity it can be. Without challenges in your life, goals cannot be achieved. If your goal is to climb the highest mountain and you happen to be afraid of heights, then your goal becomes to overcome that fear. Are you getting the idea? Goals and challenges are intertwined. You can't have one without the other.

Setting goals is the first step in achieving them. Without a mark to hit, you never really know what you're aiming for. In fact, you set goals without even realizing it. Maybe it's your goal to wake up tomorrow morning at 6:00 a.m. for work. Or perhaps you have a goal to watch the latest episode of your favorite television show this week. The truth is, you set goals every day. Goals and dreams are close relatives. If it's a dream of yours, then it automatically becomes a goal. Even a pipe dream, such as being able to fly like Superman, brings you back to that all-important question—What are you prepared to do?

Highly successful people ask this question constantly. If they have set their goals correctly, and if they are focused, the answer is always the same: "anything." So, at this point in your journey, what are *you* prepared to do?

Chapter Five

CREATE YOUR OWN LUCK

Have you ever wished for that one lucky break that would allow your dreams to become a reality or reflected upon someone's success and envied their luck? If so, you're not alone. It has almost become a cliché to say someone is lucky. There is a degree of chance that is involved in everything in life. It seems that everyone is chasing luck, but only a select few ever catch it.

A survey conducted by the Consumer Federation of America and the financial services firm Primerica revealed that 40 percent of Americans with incomes between $25,000 and $35,000—and nearly one-half of respondents with incomes of $15,000 to $25,000—thought that winning the lottery would give them their retirement funds. Overall, 27 percent of respondents said that their best chance to gain $500,000 in their lifetime was via a sweepstakes or lottery win. Even more astonishing is that this survey was conducted in 1999, during the stock market boom of the dot-com era. Untold numbers of people were becoming rich overnight by investing in the stock market or by starting up companies in their garages, yet a substantial portion of the American public still thought they could rely on luck to make themselves successful.

To become successful, you must make a decision to pursue success. You can't leave it to chance. People who have Career Intensity make personal choices that are in line with their passion, their goals, and their tolerance for risk. They break through limiting beliefs and realize that they always have choices. Before you can move forward, you must give yourself the permission and the willingness to do whatever it takes to achieve your goals. Then, when you create the conditions in your career that will help you capitalize on opportunities as they arise, you will be in the position to reap the rewards of your journey.

FOUR QUALITIES THAT ATTRACT SUCCESS

Louis Pasteur, the famous French scientist, said, "Fortune favors the prepared mind." In order to prepare yourself to welcome success, you need to replicate the mindset of high achievers and create your own luck.

Over the years, I have found that top performers—whether they were entrepreneurs, company executives, superstars of the academic world, or emerging leaders in business and public service—share four common qualities that draw opportunity toward them. Although these traits are often dismissed as being soft, they are the common denominator in those individuals who appear to be lucky, but who, in fact, attract success like a magnet. In sum, they take calculated risks; they create a positive environment for themselves and everyone around them; they work hard at making things simple; and they follow the 80/20 rule.

Take Calculated Risks

Successful people take risks—the possibility of damage, injury, or loss—in order to capitalize on opportunities. Risk-taking is a part of everyday business and everyday life. If you are a strategic thinker (as discussed in Chapter Three), you are already contemplating the potential consequences of every decision and have prepared contingency plans that you can put to work if things don't go your way.

There are certain types of risks that you can almost never proactively address. These are the risks associated with accidents, natural disasters, or another unexpected calamity. To address these issues, you transfer the risk by purchasing insurance. Superachievers have emergency plans in place to deal with the aftermaths of these types of situations. They review them on a regular basis and they assess their insurance coverage to make certain that it is up-to-date and sufficient for their needs.

The type of risk that most people and most businesses face each day is the risk involved in making decisions. This is referred to as speculative risk because the possibility exists that the outcome could be either favorable or unfavorable. The risk taker is speculating on the potential result of the decision. Successful individuals win these situations most of the time; the outcome is favorable more often than not. In order to win, they use a four-step process to aggressively evaluate each opportunity.

Assess and eliminate the risk of doing nothing. You may often sit back and wait for others to take the lead in a situation that contains an element of risk. Occasionally, the appropriate decision for a given set of circumstances is to take no action whatsoever. A top achiever is excellent at assessing whether or not action is warranted in a certain situation. She works to immediately quantify a situation and determine if doing nothing is a viable option. If it is not, she rules it out instantly. She does this even if she does not yet know what the appropriate course of action may be. She views the first step in the process of making a risky decision as deciding whether doing nothing could be an option.

List the proactive steps that could positively influence the outcome. For a successful individual, the next step in evaluating risk is to list all of the potential actions that could be taken immediately to reduce the risk of the decision. What information could he gather? How much information would he need? Who are his resources? What can he do right now to get up to speed on the situation? He lists the answers and enlists people to help in gathering the necessary information.

Live the Triple A rule—Always Avoid Assumptions. Assumptions have been the cause of more than one bad decision. A top performer does not take risks unless she has built a fact-based foundation for her decision. This intense individual always avoids assumptions—particularly when dealing with risk.

Play the odds. When making a decision, a successful individual always tries to understand the odds involved in his choice. He looks at the probability of a favorable outcome vs. an unfavorable outcome. Is there anything that can be done to increase the likelihood that the outcome will be favorable? Can he take steps to minimize the chance of unfavorable events? He only takes risks when the odds are in his favor.

Creating a Positive Environment

In discussing success with the leaders of every field of endeavor, they all mention creating a positive environment and having a positive attitude as necessary prerequisites for success. These leaders often say that most of their inner strength comes from the positive feelings they engender when doing things for others.

There are two main ingredients necessary to create a positive attitude. To truly be a positive person—a person who will welcome success and make your own luck—you must create a positive internal environment as well as a positive external environment. This means that you must not only surround yourself with positive people and reminders of your unlimited potential, but you must also master your internal self-dialogue. You cannot afford to have a single negative thought in your head. Just as negative people can drag you down, negative thoughts can become embedded in your unconscious mind and undermine your attempts at success.

People like to be around those who are kind and fair. They like to be near people who offer them hope and who view the glass as half-full instead of half-empty. People like to be around others who laugh and enjoy life. All of these things are part of having a positive attitude. In being positive, you project an image that attracts others to you.

A positive environment is one in which people feel good about themselves and the work they are doing. They enjoy working with one another and look forward to coming to work. A positive environment is one where people give of themselves not only to make money, but also because they have a sense of higher purpose—a sense that they are contributing to something that is larger than their individual needs.

One of the best ways to create a positive environment in the world around you is to give of yourself to others. Many highly successful individuals give huge sums of money to worthy charitable causes. A large number of these folks make their contributions anonymously. They do not want to be publicly recognized for their giving. They give because it makes them feel good about themselves. It helps them influence their environment in a positive way, while allowing them to give something back to the community.

Beyond making a financial contribution to a worthy cause, many top achievers give their time and expertise to others. Those who feel most fulfilled give as a part of their everyday jobs. Many business leaders view teaching as leading and they help foster a positive attitude in their organizations by requiring knowledge sharing, both formally and informally.

Kindness is a very powerful way to create a positive external environment. This is a word you do not often hear in the corporate world. It is much more popular to be a tough guy and to give the impression that you don't take any crap from people. Even though it's true that you should never allow others to take advantage of you, your family, or your company, and that you should crush your enemies, those two principles are not at odds with a philosophy of kindness. Kindness and living a positive life or career will provide you with the strength to help you defeat people who have malice in their hearts—people who want to take what you have earned.

At the end of an interview with a real estate executive who is famous for being a tough guy, I asked him about attitude, being a positive thinker, and kindness. The executive smiled and called it his secret weapon. This leader is known as a ruthless negotiator; others in his field are thoroughly intimidated when working a deal with him. Yet he said that remaining positive and optimistic kept him going during a particularly difficult period in his business and his life. This positive attitude, he acknowledged, came from doing good things for others—often anonymously. Sometimes he would do kind things for his employees, and sometimes he would do amazing things for people he did not even know.

He would not elaborate beyond that comment, but as I stood up to leave, he pulled a piece of paper from his desk. He walked with me to a copy machine, all the while talking about a business deal he was working on. He made a copy of the piece of paper and folded it in half. At that point, he leaned over and whispered in my ear—which was uncharacteristic of this usually boisterous man. He said, "I don't know who wrote this. It was given to me by a friend a long time ago when I was having a difficult time financially and personally. The moral of the story is something that I keep in mind every day. I realized that, if I approached my interactions with people while keeping this story in mind, my problems would solve themselves."

The business giant then handed me the paper, spun around, and walked down the hall bellowing for one of his assistants to get an associate on the phone. I was stunned. Here is the story that was on the paper he handed me:

Twenty years ago, I drove a cab for a living. It was a cowboy's life, a life for someone who wanted no boss. What I didn't realize was that it was also a ministry.

Because I drove the night shift, my cab became a moving confessional. Passengers climbed in, sat behind me in total anonymity, and told me about their lives. I encountered people whose lives amazed me, ennobled me, made me laugh, and weep. But none touched me more than a woman I picked up late one August night.

I was responding to a call from a small brick fourplex in a quiet part of town. I assumed I was being sent to pick up some partiers, or someone who had just had a fight with a lover, or a worker heading to an early shift at some factory in the industrial part of town.

When I arrived at 2:30 a.m., the building was dark except for a single light in a ground-floor window. Under these circumstances, many drivers would just honk once or twice, wait a minute, and then drive away. But I had seen too many impoverished people who depended on taxis as their only means of transportation. Unless a situation smelled of danger, I always went to the door. This passenger might be someone who needs my assistance, I reasoned to myself. So I walked to the door and knocked.

"Just a minute," answered a frail, elderly voice. I could hear something being dragged across the floor. After a long pause, the door opened. A small woman in her 80s stood before me. She was wearing a print dress and a pillbox hat with a veil pinned on it, like somebody out of a 1940s movie.

By her side was a small nylon suitcase. The apartment looked as if no one had lived in it for years. All the furniture was covered with sheets. There were no clocks on the walls, and no knick-knacks or utensils on the counters. In the corner was a cardboard box filled with photos and glassware.

"Would you carry my bag out to the car?" she said. I took the suitcase to the cab, then returned to assist the woman. She took my arm and we walked slowly toward the curb. She kept thanking me for my kindness.

"It's nothing," I told her. "I just try to treat my passengers the way I would want my mother treated."

"Oh, you're such a good boy," she said.

When we got in the cab, she gave me an address, then asked, "Could you drive through downtown?"

"It's not the shortest way," I answered quickly.

"Oh, I don't mind," she said. "I'm in no hurry. I'm on my way to a hospice."

I looked in the rearview mirror. Her eyes were glistening.

"I don't have any family left," she continued. "The doctor says I don't have very long."

I quietly reached over and shut off the meter. "What route would you like me to take?" I asked.

For the next two hours, we drove through the city. She showed me the building where she had once worked as an elevator operator. We drove through the neighborhood where she and her husband had lived when they were newlyweds. She had me pull up in front of a furniture warehouse that had once been a ballroom where she had gone dancing as a girl. Sometimes she'd ask me to slow in front of a particular building or corner and would sit staring into the darkness, saying nothing.

As the first hint of sun was creasing the horizon, she suddenly said, "I'm tired. Let's go now."

We drove in silence to the address she had given me. It was a low building, like a small convalescent home, with a driveway that passed under a portico. Two orderlies came out to the cab as soon as we pulled up. They were solicitous and intent, watching her every move. They must have been expecting her.

I opened the trunk and took the small suitcase to the door. The woman was already seated in a wheelchair.

"How much do I owe you?" she asked, reaching into her purse.

"Nothing," I said.

"You have to make a living," she answered.

"There are other passengers," I responded.

Almost without thinking, I bent and gave her a hug. She held onto me tightly.

"You gave an old woman a little moment of joy," she said.
"Thank you."
I squeezed her hand, then walked into the dim morning light.
Behind me, a door shut. It was the sound of the closing of a life.
I didn't pick up any more passengers that shift. I drove aim-
lessly, lost in thought. For the rest of that day, I could hardly talk.
What if that woman had gotten an angry driver, or one who was
impatient to end his shift? What if I had refused to take the run, or
had honked once, then driven away?

On a quick review, I don't think that I have done anything
more important in my life. We're conditioned to think that our
lives revolve around great moments. But great moments often
catch us unaware—beautifully wrapped in what others may consider a small one.

People don't remember exactly what you did, or what you
said . . . but they will always remember how you made them feel.

—Author Unknown

Making people feel good or valued is not something that is
taught in business schools, yet it is central to maintaining a positive
attitude and making your own luck. Successful individuals make
people feel good about themselves and this feeling is reflected back
to them many times over. In business and in life, you deal with people who you do not like. Most often, you do so because you have
to. After an experience with a negative person, you walk away
thinking that you will avoid another interaction with him using any
means necessary. From a purely business perspective, how much
has the negativity of that one person cost that business?

Although many people are negative and cynical, they are not
born that way. Often, people develop a negative outlook by allowing the events of the day or life's obstacles to interfere with their
inherent positive natures.

Everyone has the potential to regain a positive attitude. For
many people, finding optimism comes from recalling why they
originally entered their chosen field. That was certainly the case
with Marc Raymond. Marc is a Web designer at Columbia University. He had long held the desire to work in the media, but he
had become cynical and disaffected with what he was doing.
Here's his story:

When I grew up in Rhode Island, Chuck Barris—the host of *The Gong Show*—was one of my heroes. Other kids had Reggie Jackson, Carl Yastrzemski, or Spiderman. I had Chuck Barris. For me, Chuck was a wizard of fun. He was a catalyst for craziness. I went right from *Sesame Street* to *The Gong Show*. *The Gong Show* was my favorite show because it was like a living cartoon. You had all of these people just being themselves and it was great. In January of 2003, I was doing Web design and I wasn't really satisfied with what I was doing. I was really disillusioned with media and with my job as a whole. In fact, I was thinking about leaving my job and going to art school.

One night, on my way home from work, I got a call from my wife and she told me that Chuck Barris was at the local Barnes & Noble, signing books. His book, *Confessions of a Dangerous Mind: An Unauthorized Autobiography*, had just come out. I met my wife there, we listened to Chuck speak, and I was riveted. After he was done speaking, I got to talk with Chuck and he signed a book for me. I thanked him for the entertainment and inspiration he provided me when I was growing up.

As I was on my way back home, it hit me. I had this new sense of enthusiasm. I realized that the artist that I wanted to be was really inside of me all along. I began to understand that I didn't need to go to art school to realize my dream. I understood that it was as much about the journey as it was about the destination. It was right there that I understood that I wanted to do something with my talent that would benefit other people.

I view my work at Columbia as a positive force. I help enable the learning of others. This is truly a good use of the Internet, and I am happy about that. I also know that since I enrolled in the strategic communications program at Columbia, I'll be able to continue to use my talent to help other people realize their dreams.

Now when there are days that I don't feel that my attitude is exactly as positive as it should be, I look at my autographed copy of Chuck's book. In it he wrote, "Marc, quit your day job." That inscription always takes me back and helps me remember why I got involved in media in the first place—to make a difference in people's lives.

By interacting with one of his childhood heroes, Marc was able to recall what energized him about being involved in the media. This restored his positive attitude and inspired him to follow a dream that he is passionate about.

Many people have stories like Marc's. When you feel yourself becoming negative about a situation or a job, think back to the point when you first got involved in that activity. Relive the moment or moments in as much detail as possible. If you can recapture the positive feelings and energy that you had during that time, try to find a way to incorporate them into your current activities. If you can't do that, you should find something else to do—something that makes you feel good and allows you to be positive each day.

There are times when your negative feelings are deeply rooted in your subconscious. Being kind and doing good deeds will certainly help you feel better about the world around you and create an externally positive environment. But you must also work hard to make certain that you are influencing your subconscious. One of the best ways to do this is through positive affirmations. Even though they're often dismissed as New Age techniques, affirmations really do help you reprogram your subconscious mind to eliminate the negative self-talk that can undermine your success. Develop your own positive affirmations and give them a try for just 30 days. It will make a difference in the way you feel about yourself and your life.

Affirmations must be based in a truth related to your life. If you are unable to believe your statement, on some level, your mind will work against your efforts and cancel out any potentially positive change. You don't need to believe every affirmation completely, though. Since you are trying to reprogram your negative subconscious, there will naturally be resistance to your positive affirmation statement.

Let's examine creating an affirmation you could use to develop a more positive attitude towards your ability to make business deals. You could use the simple affirmation, "I am a good negotiator." Even though this may not always feel accurate, you know that it is true, at least sometimes. If you have made one deal that you feel was positive, then at least that one time you were a good negotiator. Deep down, you know that you have the ability to make more deals like that. You really are a good negotiator. It is important that you believe your statement, at least on an intellectual level. Ultimately, you agree with this affirmation. This is critical. The main reason negative thoughts create negative results is that you agree with them. Your objective is to shift your mental focus away from the negative thoughts and toward the positive thoughts.

Your mind is critical by nature. This means that it naturally criticizes your own thinking. When negative thoughts come up, accept them as natural because that is the way the brain was designed to work. Do not, however, give these thoughts any additional attention. Imagine them evaporating into thin air, like a puff of smoke. For example, if the thought, "I am not a good negotiator because I overpaid for my car" comes up, just let it go. Simply because a thought is in your head does not mean it is true.

Resistance will often cause negative thoughts to persist. If someone were to say to you, "You are a small gray squirrel," you would probably not be insulted (you might be confused, but not insulted) because your brain would not examine this statement critically. There is no basis for it in reality. Even if you thought to yourself, "I might be a small gray squirrel," that thought would just evaporate. This is exactly how you want your brain to handle negative thoughts. Now, if someone came up to you and said, "You are a bad negotiator because you didn't receive a signing bonus when you took your job," you could become very upset. This is because, somewhere in your mind, you may feel that you have failed in your responsibility to yourself and your family when you took your job. At some level, you agree with that statement.

This is precisely the problem. You mind will now begin a self-dialogue of arguing both sides of this issue. In reality, you made a mistake, but that does not make you a bad negotiator. That is one incident, isolated in time. It is over. It's in your past. Having the internal argument with yourself will allow the negative thought to exist in your mind for an indefinite period of time. The best thing to do is to acknowledge that your mind is beginning to have this internal dialogue and then let the whole thing rise up and evaporate. Say to yourself, "That is my mind just doing its job—being critical—let it go." Your mind is in the business of helping existing thoughts survive. Once you command it to let those thoughts go, you will need to replace them with new thoughts.

Now, let's say you want to create a positive attitude toward your new career as an Entrepreneur. You begin with the affirmation, "I am a positive force in the world."

Then, notice what comes up. You will probably get a negative response. Just write it down or say it out loud. You might come up with, "I am a positive, powerful business giant. That's not true. I'm just starting my business, and I'm scared to death."

Acknowledge your response; there is negativity in there that needs to be released. Once you fully experience the feeling, it has served its purpose and is then free to dissipate. That is just the way the mind works. Take a deep breath and allow the negative feelings and thoughts to present themselves. Then, as you exhale, watch them evaporate into thin air. Now take another breath and say (or write) the positive affirmation again. This time think about some of the positive things you have done in the past 24 hours. Replay them in your mind, remembering every detail. If the events were directed toward yourself, recreate the feeling of positive accomplishment as you repeat to yourself, "I am a positive, powerful business giant." Allow the feelings of success and happiness to wash over you as you reflect upon the positive steps you have taken in creating your new business, and the positive things you will do in the upcoming days and weeks. If negative thoughts reenter, acknowledge them and allow them to dissipate.

As you practice this positive affirmation process, you will notice it becomes second nature. You will begin to improve your internal dialogue, and it will begin to affect your external personality. With the practice that comes from focusing your thinking, you will become a more positive person. Even though some people dismiss the process of creating positive affirmations as New Age, most successful people just look at it as a way to control and influence their thinking in a positive way.

Establishing a positive environment is a critical component for personal success. Once you have established an environment that allows you to take an optimistic view toward everything in your life, you will have to work hard to maintain that environment. Even though there are many ways to work at maintaining a positive outlook, I've found a few to be particularly helpful.

Each day, take 15 minutes to write at least one note to someone in your address book or e-mail contact list. In this handwritten note, make sure you identify something that you like about them and at least one reason why you are grateful for them being associated with you. Not only are most people genuinely touched when they receive such a note, but the process of writing it allows you to reflect on the positive aspects of your relationship with this particular person. When you engage in this process:

Keep it clean. Make sure you don't have an ulterior motive or hidden agenda. If you do have an agenda, don't write a brief handwritten note. Instead, use traditional business correspondence and state your purpose for writing—your agenda—right up front.

Make sure it's handwritten. Handwritten notes are personal, so make sure you write clearly and from the heart. Do not be afraid to express some emotion. Things like "Your comments at our recent meeting really made me feel good about our friendship," are not inappropriate.

Use regular mail and buy a real stamp. When your note arrives, it will appear less formal and more personal. This will show that you cared enough to take time out of your day to buy a stamp and walk to a mailbox.

Keep it short. Don't use this as an opportunity to pour your heart out. All that is necessary is a few lines to let the recipient know that you find him valuable.

Another way to maintain a positive attitude is to hold a Gratitude Visit, a technique developed by Dr. Martin Seligman, considered the father of positive psychology. In his book, *Authentic Happiness* (Free Press, 2002), Seligman outlines how he and his students have used this powerful tool. His book is a great resource for people who need a jump-start on a positive outlook toward life.

When I conduct my gratitude visits, I start by writing a letter to a person who has had a dramatic, positive impact on my life. I put the letter in a nice frame and I schedule a time to meet for a cup of coffee. I let her know that I just want to spend some time catching up. Then I go to see her and I give her the letter and let her know why I am grateful for her support. Sometimes I read the letter verbatim, while at other times, we talk about some past happy moments. The point is to thank the person for what she has done for you in the past. Try at least one gratitude visit yourself. I promise it will improve your attitude and the attitude of the person you visit.

A third way to develop a positive attitude is also adapted from Dr. Seligman's work. At night, before going to sleep, reflect back upon your day. Focus on three things that went right and discuss them with your partner. Having an internal dialogue is fine, but discussing something out loud makes it that much more powerful. Next, discuss three things for which you feel grateful. Finally, discuss three action items that you will work on during the day tomorrow. As you discuss them, picture yourself completing those tasks. When describing your action items, the more detail you provide, the sharper the images will appear in your mind. After doing this every night for a couple of weeks, you will feel energized and alive when you start each day. This exercise only takes fifteen minutes each day, but it will change your life!

Working Hard to Make Things Simple

Have you ever met someone who loves to complicate things? He relishes showing you how smart he is by making a concept or procedure so difficult that only he can understand it. This person doesn't get very far in business and often becomes a politician. In truth, it is much more difficult to simplify than it is to complicate. Although the word "simple" often gets a bad rap since it is often used synonymously with "inferior" and "substandard," making things simple is one of the qualities that can help you create your own luck.

You have already simplified your life by creating and focusing on your goals. This will help you streamline your approach toward your career. Simplicity plays an important role in creating luck through your interactions with others. There are three ways successful people make sure their relationships are uncomplicated.

Exercise common sense. Don't impose unrealistic expectations on others. If you ask someone to complete a task for you, first make certain that it is possible. It can be a challenge, but it must be possible. Next, make certain that it is ethical. You should never ask someone to do anything that would in any way compromise your integrity or hers. Finally, ask yourself if you can live with the most extreme results of your requests or actions. Common sense in dealing with other people is the best way to keep things simple and a great way to draw in your own luck.

Maintain an external orientation. Always try to see things from the other point of view. It's easy to get caught up in your own agenda and fail to see how the other person may view your behavior or actions. A successful person—someone with Career Intensity—views the world with an external orientation. He examines each action from the perspective of an outsider. This helps give him a clear picture of the issue at hand before he proceeds. He checks his ego at the door, and he takes the best course of action— not just because it is best for him, but because it is also the right thing to do.

Remember that wishing doesn't make things happen. Hope is a great tool for staying optimistic and positive, but achieving your goals requires action. Do not make decisions based upon things that you hope will happen. Make decisions based upon concrete evidence, past precedents, or the resources that are available. Keep wishful thinking out of the decision-making process. You will thank yourself later.

FOLLOW THE 80/20 RULE

Many people call the 80/20 rule The Pareto Principle since it is often attributed to Italian economist Vilfredo Pareto. He created a mathematical formula to describe the unequal distribution of wealth in his country (as measured by land ownership). Pareto observed that 20 percent of the people owned 80 percent of the land. In the late 1940s, Dr. Joseph Juran took Pareto's name and his description of the economic state of Italy in 1906 and used it to describe his "theory of the vital few and the trivial many."

The underlying theory is that a few (20 percent) greatly influence the outcome of a situation, and the many (80 percent) have a limited impact. When he applied this theory to manufacturing, Juran discovered that 20 percent of the defects in products were causing 80 percent of the problems for customers. In working on a project, you can almost always predict that 20 percent of the work (the first 10 percent and the last 10 percent) will take up 80 percent of your time. There are literally hundreds of examples of the few requiring more resources than the many.

Although this law should not be interpreted literally, a successful individual uses it to her advantage every day. She focuses her time and effort on the vital few things that influence the greatest results. She uses this as a form of mental leverage. She focuses on the most productive aspects of everything she does and works around or delegates the least productive aspects of her work. Perhaps the greatest proof of this principle lies in your own life. Think back to something that you are particularly proud to have accomplished. On a sheet of paper, write down all the tasks that you performed in order to bring about this achievement. As you look at those tasks, think about those that were high-value tasks and those that you could have avoided. You will find that consistent effort focused on a few critical tasks helped you achieve your desired results.

The best way to use this principle in a forward-looking manner is to examine any particularly difficult task on which you're currently working. Look closely at the desired outcome and make a list of the steps necessary to achieve that result. As you look over your list, analyze which tasks will provide you with the best results (both in quality and quantity). Once you have determined which tasks are the vital few, attack them with all of your effort. You will often find that the momentum of attacking the most critical items at the beginning of a project will help sustain your effort to complete the project in a shorter time period than you originally anticipated.

Sales professionals often talk in great detail about the 80/20 rule. They regularly tell stories of how 80 percent of their business comes from 20 percent of their customers. People often encourage them not to waste their time with the remaining 80 percent, but to focus on the 20 percent that drives their business. This could lead to trouble. Even though you focus on the 20 percent of the customers that *currently* provide 80 percent of the value in your portfolio, you need to make certain that *someone* is mining the 80 percent to look for additions to your 20 percent. In other words, you must continually work to enlarge the pie, rather than take a larger percentage of the smaller, existing pie. For example, 20 percent of 300 is double the size of 30 percent of 100.

The 80/20 rule will continue to work for you if you always look to enlarge the universe in which you are striving to achieve the 20 percent share. You need to be creative and always expand your operating universe.

Chapter Six

PREPARE FOR EVERY INTERACTION

If you've ever sat in a meeting letting your mind go numb as your colleague drones on and watching the clock as the minutes tick by, you've given away part of your life that you'll never regain. If you've ever had a chance encounter with the president of your company or a mover and shaker at a rival company and found yourself tongue-tied, you've missed a golden opportunity to shine. Whenever you have an interaction in which you're present in body but not in spirit, you have no control over the outcome and won't benefit from the encounter.

Implementing outcome-driven thinking, as discussed in Chapter Two, involves preparing for every interaction. People with Career Intensity focus their preparation just as a detective focuses as he builds a case. They spend the time necessary to develop a solid understanding of the desired outcomes for each party in each situation. This preparation allows them to anticipate the needs of the other party and to develop a deep and lasting relationship, the rewards of which they will continue to reap over time.

Each interaction you have with another person represents an opportunity. At a minimum, you have an opportunity to build a relationship. Interactions with others are black and white. They either have a positive outcome, or they have a negative outcome. There are no neutral interactions.

One quality that separates people who have outstanding careers from those whose careers fail to live up to their expectations is preparation. Successful people are always well prepared. The

most successful individuals even appear to be prepared for seemingly random encounters.

THE THREE RULES OF ENGAGEMENT

The interaction of your goals with your strategic mindset will help
define the meetings you plan. Once the meetings are set, you need
to have a clear understanding of your desired outcome and how
you can best achieve that result. Preparation allows you to understand the goals of the other party participating in the meeting. The
greater your ability to help them achieve their objectives, the more
likely they will help you achieve your goals.

For each interaction you have with other people, you should
follow the Three Rules of Engagement: know yourself; investigate
your target; and define and execute a plan of attack.

Know Yourself

The critical first step in preparation is understanding what you
want to gain from an interaction or a meeting. Pinpoint your goal
for the encounter. If you do not have a desired outcome in mind,
do not schedule the meeting in the first place. In business, time is
a precious and finite commodity. Right now, make the commitment not to schedule a meeting without first knowing your objective for the meeting.

Next, list both acceptable and unacceptable topics for discussion during the meeting. You should craft a message that you want
to convey to the other party (your target). What do you want them
to know about you? If you could only convey one thing to the
other side in this meeting, what would it be? Everyone from your
team who attends the meeting should know this message and not
stray from it.

Knowing yourself (your company and your team) is an important part of the preparation equation, but it is only the first part.
You also need to think about the other side—let's call them the
target—and what they will want to convey.

I am very fortunate to have fine people working with me who
help me prepare for each meeting I attend. We follow a simple pro-

cedure when we set up a meeting or accept a meeting invitation. We ask the other participant what he would like to get out of our meeting, and we clearly state our desired outcome. We do this over the phone and then follow up with a note—usually an e-mail—to reinforce the points. The pre-meeting note process serves several purposes: It helps keep my team focused; it demonstrates respect for the time of everyone involved in the meeting; it clears up any ambiguity between the two parties as to why the meeting is taking place; and it reinforces my own personal brand in the mind of the person with whom I am meeting.

As an aside, experience has shown that if you communicate with someone three times within a short time frame—two weeks—they are far more likely to remember you than if you communicate with them only once. In the case of meeting preparation, the phone call to identify outcomes for the meeting is the first communication. The e-mail is the second. The pre-meeting handwritten note (if the meeting is in the distant future), or the meeting itself is the third communication. Add to those three a thank-you note and a post-meeting phone call (with a question you "just thought of"), and you have made an indelible impression in the mind of your target.

As you prepare for the meeting, you are essentially conducting an investigation. You are looking for patterns of behavior and commonality between your company and the company with whom you are meeting. You are also seeking to discover complementary aspects of your relationship. Establishing commonality is great for building rapport and sharing best practices, while pinpointing complementary qualities serves to establish a synergistic relationship—one in which you can leverage each other's strengths for a mutually beneficial outcome.

Most of the information you need in your investigative phase is available using two types of research: primary research and secondary research. Primary research consists of direct contact or firsthand experience in gathering the information. Secondary research consists of gathering information from third-party sources, such as the Internet, public records, and books as well as magazines.

You will sometimes hear this process referred to as "due diligence," which we use here to mean investigating everything. People often bristle at the thought of conducting due diligence before something as simple as a meeting. However, this is one of the practices that separates those who are good from those who are great.

Contrary to its name, secondary research should be performed first. Start by developing a plan of attack in which you jot down the information you need in order to knowledgeably speak to your counterpart about her industry and company. Next, think of the most accessible places to find this information. Don't just head to the Internet and begin searching aimlessly or meeting preparation will become a full-time job. On your list, make notes as to the type of sites that may have the information you need.

Your secondary research should help you develop a framework for formulating questions that you can ask a company representative prior to your meeting. It must reveal a potentially achievable outcome for you when you meet with this company. A good test for this is to answer the following two questions: Who in the target company can help you achieve your objective, and how will this meeting bring you closer to your goal?

If your secondary research adequately addresses these areas, you may not need to conduct primary research prior to your meeting. Time permitting, though, it is always a good idea to continue on and explore these areas more deeply.

Before a meeting, the most effective way to perform primary research is to conduct interviews with people who have worked with your target or to conduct an interview with the target company itself.

If the meeting happens to be a sales meeting or one where the objective is to get the other party to take action, it is best to try to gather direct intelligence. Superachievers take a consultative approach to intelligence gathering. My team has learned a great deal from observing them, and we have developed an effective pre-meeting process. This consultative model has worked for us in many different fields over the years.

When someone inquires about our services, we ask permission to interview her to help us understand her needs. We have developed a detailed phone interview that lasts about 30 minutes and allows us to thoroughly prepare for a meeting based upon the prospective client's business situation. This also helps establish rapport with the client prior to the time when we enter the meeting room. The interview can be done with one of the meeting attendees or with someone who is familiar with the prospective client's desired outcome. If the interviewee is not sure what the prospect would like to get out of the meeting, then some general questions about the overall health of the organization—with a particular focus on the meeting attendee's area—are usually most effective. Following are interview questions that can lead to a healthy understanding of your prospect and her business:

What are your company's goals this year?

What are your biggest challenges?

What are your key initiatives for the next one to two years?

Is there consensus among your executive team about your company's strategic vision and direction?

What are you doing to align the performance of your frontline managers and employees with your corporate goals and strategic initiatives?

How are these managers and employees evaluated and held accountable for their performances?

What are you doing to improve the performance of your managers and employees?

How effective is the development of your managers and employees?

What kind of experience do you want your customers to have?

What do your customers think of you?

Describe your best customer.

Describe your typical customer.

How do these two customers differ?

How are you helping your managers and employees consistently deliver a remarkable experience?

Are your managers and employees held accountable for how well they deliver this customer experience?

What are your goals for the next one to two years?

Who in your business/industry do you most admire? Why?

Tell me the best success story from your business. How can you create more experiences like that?

Tell me about the social network in your organization. How do you get the word out about a new idea?

What keeps you awake at night?

What are your key criteria for establishing a new business relationship?

This pre-meeting planning provides you with significant value in four specific ways. First, it creates a positive impression upon the people with whom you are meeting. Taking time to understand someone and his business is flattering and communicates that you take him seriously. Asking good, thoughtful questions is a sign of intelligence and respect, an impression that you definitely want to create in the mind of a potential friend or business partner.

Second, thorough planning serves as a catalyst for new ideas and new ways to approach the meeting topic. Often, those on one side of an issue can fall victim to groupthink, which arises when a group of people with shared perspectives and experiences continually draw from the same well of ideas. Asking questions of the meeting participants ahead of time often ignites new ideas within you or your team and is likely to spark ideas from the other side as well. Such pre-planning sets the stage for a more productive exchange when everyone is in the room together.

Third, advanced planning provides you with an advantage over any competition you may have. Any time you have the opportunity to interact with the client, you come away with information that your competition may not have or may not have thought to look for. At the very least, you will have developed rapport before you enter a meeting. If your competition also diligently prepares for their meeting, then this process is critical for you to keep up. If they have not prepared in this way, then you are far ahead of them.

Fourth, pre-planning helps you understand the perspective of the people with whom you will be meeting. Once you understand their perspective, you are better able to set actionable goals and craft an effective message for the meeting.

Investigate Your Target

Your meeting has been set and you have a prospect or a target in mind. You have conducted preliminary research to prepare your own position. You now need to put yourself in your target's shoes in order to help you prepare for any questions or issues that may arise, as well as to help refine your approach to presenting information to the other party.

The best way to get inside your target's mind is to approach the process as though you were a detective trying to solve a case. When building his case, a good detective looks for three elements: motivation, means, and opportunity.

Motivation refers to the reason why the other party would request or attend a meeting with you. If you understand the motivation of the other side, you immediately have a lever you can use to help get what you want from the meeting. Essentially, you are looking for a problem that you can help that other organization solve.

When it comes to motivation, you should try and find answers to the following questions: What do they want? Are their goals in alignment with ours? Is there a way we can meet their needs and achieve our objective?

If you are meeting with a person or an organization that has a specific problem, and you have a solution to that problem, your value to that person is high. If your value to your target is high, then you will have a greater opportunity to get what you want out of the meeting. Research is critical to the preparation for any meeting because finding a problem to solve—finding the motivation—is essential.

What means does your target have to achieve his objective? Specifically, what resources are available to him? Are there any missing resources that are necessary for the target to achieve his goal? Can you be the means to provide those resources? When you research the means, you can define your role in solving the problem and will be perceived as valuable by your target.

The final area of research is opportunity. What opportunity is your target assessing? Why does he feel that these opportunities are great? How is he attempting to capture these opportunities? How can you help him in his quest? Can you source other opportunities for him?

Understanding the motivation, means, and opportunity of your target is essential. At a minimum, such an understanding will help you set a framework for your discussion. Beyond that, it can be a determining factor in driving your relationship forward.

Define and Execute a Plan of Attack

Now you have all the information you need for your meeting with your target. You understand your objectives, you've crafted a message, and you have a handle on the motivation, means, and opportunity of your target. The next step is to put together a plan for the meeting itself.

This plan can be as simple as jotting some information on a piece of paper and sharing it with your team members, or it can be as complex as scripting out the entire meeting as if it were a play. The level of depth depends upon your mastery of the information and the amount of time you have to prepare.

A good meeting plan has three key elements: an objective, an agenda that your side wants to advance, and a call to action.

The meeting objective is what you want to accomplish. This should be at the forefront of your mind before and during the meeting. You should be focused on this objective the entire time you are with your target.

Your agenda should include the steps that may be necessary for you to lead up to achieving your objective. What conversation topics must be covered prior to achieving your objective in this meeting?

Finally, there should be a call to action. In a sales meeting, the call to action is to ask for the business. In a negotiation, the call to action may be to get the target to disclose some critical information necessary to make an offer (or the offer itself). In any case, before you enter the room, you must be clear on the call to action. If you've done your research, you will know your target well and can maneuver the meeting to a successful call to action.

Once the meeting is over, you should sit down with your team for a debriefing. Determine what went well and what did not occur as planned. Map out the next steps that must be taken and who will take them. You should also identify two or three specifics that you would like to improve for the next meeting. This can be particularly helpful if you attend several meetings in similar industries or with similar targets.

Although it seems like a great deal of work, meeting preparation is critical to the success of any individual or team. People with Career Intensity view this level of preparation as a competitive advantage. World-class organizations and individuals prepare with this level of detail for every encounter—including those that appear to be random.

Mastering the Random Encounter

When was the last time you went to Starbucks for a cup of coffee? I was just there this morning . . . and yesterday . . . and the day before that. Yes, I am addicted to caffeine, but that's not the reason I keep going back to Starbucks. Where you buy your coffee could advance your career.

Starbucks has a powerful brand that attracts people to its shops like magnets. This attraction does not discriminate. Just about everybody goes to Starbucks. Smart people. Rich people. Successful people. They all head in to this welcoming environment to get their shot of caffeine prepared just the way they like it. Some people rush in and rush out. Others hang around to read or work. Some people meet their friends and talk.

The one thing that virtually every customer at Starbucks has in common is that each person orders a drink that has to be made by someone behind the counter. This process is unavoidable and, under the most ideal circumstances, it takes at least two minutes. This two-minute time period represents a moment of opportunity—and possibly the opportunity of a lifetime.

My recent experience at Starbucks is a good illustration. I'm waiting for my Venti Vanilla Skim Cappuccino and I notice that I'm standing next to a well-dressed woman holding a legal brief. It just so happens that I need to consult with an intellectual property attorney on some content rights for my blog, and I'm having a difficult time finding someone who specializes in Internet law. I make eye contact with my fellow coffee drinker and say, "Hi. I noticed that you are carrying a legal brief. I'm currently looking for some advice and I wonder if you know of a good intellectual property lawyer?" She says she does know a few but their specialties vary. I hand her my card and I ask her to pass my information along to the people she knows. She says she is happy to do so.

My nonthreatening approach led to a brief conversation that ended when she received her coffee and walked out the door. She subsequently e-mailed me with some helpful information, and I not only found a great intellectual property attorney, but I also used her firm for a real estate matter.

The key factors that make Starbucks the perfect place for maximizing the opportunity of a random encounter include:

- You and the person you would like to meet have a common purpose: waiting for a drink. Having something in common subconsciously builds rapport.
- The encounter has a definite ending. You receive your drink and you're gone, or the other person receives his drink and he's gone.
- The time period is just long enough to make a significant point, but not long enough to get sucked in.
- For an ever-so-brief period, your audience is captive—they paid for their drink and they need to wait to receive it.
- Overall, people don't have their guard up in a casual environment, and they welcome a distraction from their wait.

Although you may come into contact with hundreds of people each day in "Starbucks Moments," you may never have considered leveraging those interactions to your benefit. These encounters are the perfect example of a phenomenon of potential interaction that could be a catalyst for positive change in your life. It is possible to master encounters that appear to occur randomly. You interact with people each day that can help you achieve your goals. You need only to be prepared for the critical conversations.

In order to be effective in this type of environment, you need to hone your Starbucks Speech. If you had to convince your client or your boss to buy your solution during the time it takes to make a Caramel Macchiato, could you do it? You must develop the ability to get your point across in a concise way under time pressure. For the random encounter, you should have a number of icebreakers in your arsenal, as well as ideas for potential interactions.

Chance random encounters can be beneficial, but planned random encounters can have an even bigger payoff. You need to prepare for your interactions in advance and then make those interactions happen. The future is too valuable to be left to chance. Starbucks can provide us with another valuable lesson, this time in the potential for a seemingly random encounter.

My office is in one of the buildings that make up the Rockefeller Center Office Complex. This is a group of office buildings that surrounds the famous skating rink in midtown Manhattan. The buildings in a seven-square block area are connected by a system of tunnels. Those tunnels contain stores, restaurants, and yes, two Starbucks. There are over 1,000 companies with 300,000 employees in the complex. Rockefeller Center is also the powerbroker capital of the world for both the print and broadcast media. The companies whose offices connect through these tunnels include NBC, CNN, Fox News Channel, Simon & Schuster, McGraw-Hill, Time-Life Publications, and Sirius Satellite Radio. It is not uncommon to see popular and well-known personalities wandering the halls, looking for a quick sandwich or yes, even buying a cup of coffee.

It occurred to me that if I wanted to meet a particular individual from one of those companies, I could put my Starbucks Speech and random encounter theory to the test, all at the same time. I set up shop at various times of the day, alternating Starbucks locations in the Rockefeller Center underground plaza. The number of powerful and influential people I recognized during this time period was staggering. I lost count at 223—and these were just people I recognized from TV appearances and the trade press. There were probably dozens of additional people with whom I interacted that were powerful and influential, but whom I didn't recognize.

Some of these people were just grabbing a quick cup of coffee and running back to their busy days. Others were popping in to get a quick break from the frantic pace of their offices. Some made small talk with the staff or the other customers. Others just came and went in the short time it took to prepare their drinks. My point was made: If I had a specific purpose for having a "random encounter" with one of these people, the opportunity would certainly present itself in one of those locations. I needed to be ready.

I am not advocating that you become a Starbucks Stalker and pester people at every opportunity. Although this technique works at Starbucks, it also works wherever you meet people who can positively impact your career or business.

You can make random encounters happen. Somebody knows someone who works with the person you want to meet. To have the opportunity to try out your Starbucks Speech, you need to find out where you can have two minutes to deliver it. Where does the person eat lunch? Where does she get her coffee? What clubs does she belong to? What charities does she volunteer to work with? These are all great places for the random encounter. You need to do your homework and have your speech ready.

When taking advantage of the random encounter, there are four steps you should take for maximum effectiveness and to keep from being punched in the nose:

1. **Allow the other person to assume a position of power.**
   When you ask for advice, directions, or even something as simple as the time, who has the power? The person providing the information has the power and control of the interaction. They can walk away or refuse to answer. Most people, when they have control of a situation, are immediately more comfortable and less intimidated—which means they are more likely to be open and receptive. I have seen frantic businesspeople rushing to meetings on the streets of New York City stop and spend ten minutes explaining to a tourist how to get to a landmark.
2. **Establish common ground.** You can do this by talking about a third party, a neutral subject, or an experience that everyone can relate to. The key here is to establish some

sort of small emotional connection with the other person. You want them to feel what you feel.

3. **Compliment them and ask for some harmless information.** You have now exchanged at least two sentences with the other person. The next step is to make him feel good. Say something like, "I could not help but admire your watch. Did you pick it because it is functional or because it looks great?" Now you should be off to the races. The idea is to get them to give you advice. Eventually you can introduce a question about where they work and what they do into the conversation.

4. **The "By the way."** After you have had your two-minute conversation and you prepare to leave, say something like, "Oh, by the way, my name is Dave," and offer your hand for a handshake. Then you can say, "May I call you if I need some advice on _____?" They will most often respond affirmatively. If they don't, just give them your business card and say that you enjoyed speaking with them.

Whether your interaction takes the form of a meeting or a random encounter, it pays to be prepared. The more opportunities you create that will help you achieve your goals, the more quickly you will realize your dreams.

Chapter Seven

MASTER PERCEPTION

If you're a Workplace Warrior—you put in your time on the job, but you don't feel passionate about your work—you're probably perceived by your coworkers, supervisor, and customers as dependable but unremarkable. If you're a Management Maverick—you implement solutions without the support of your coworkers, supervisor, and customers—you're likely perceived as a rogue. Each of these perceptions damages your career and prevents you from fulfilling your potential.

Highly successful Intrepreneurs and Entrepreneurs use others' perceptions to their advantage. By creating their own personal brand and marketing themselves—much in the same way companies position themselves and their products in the marketplace—people with Career Intensity increase the perception of their value in the minds of those they serve.

When you use personal branding to define yourself in the marketplace—either within your company or as the head of your own company—you differentiate yourself from your competition by creating value for those who use your services. Through value creation and demonstration, you will create a demand for your services, which ultimately will attract success.

THE IMPORTANCE OF PERCEPTION

A brand is the perception of a product or service in the mind of the consumer. Each of us has our own personal brand. Each of our target audiences has a perception of us. Sometimes this perception is exactly what we want it to be, and it serves us well; other times, this perception is dramatically different from how we wish to be seen and works to our detriment.

Companies take great care and spend millions upon millions of dollars to influence the perception of their target audiences. They conduct sophisticated research studies and test and retest all forms of marketing communications. They craft exactly the right message and precisely select the correct medium to reach a specific audience in the appropriate way.

Does all of this care and dedication make a difference? Absolutely! We often subscribe to the point of view the marketing professionals want us to believe. In many cases, we have no choice since we are bombarded by a variety of marketing communications about a product or service. Television commercials, billboards, direct mail brochures, radio ads, magazine ads, newspaper ads, product placement, celebrity endorsements, and sports sponsorships constantly assault us. Aggressive public relations professionals are pitching stories right now that will shape tomorrow's news. Buzz marketing companies are working over your friends and relatives to get them to recommend their products and services to you. It's no wonder that most kids can name 20 different types of candy, but they can't name five presidents of the United States. The candy gets more media attention.

So what does all of this have to do with you and your mission to develop a Career Intensity? Everything! You need to start managing yourself and your career as a brand. You need to consider the perception of your target audience before you craft a message. You need to make certain that your target audience sees you exactly the way you want them to.

Personal branding is not designed to help you create a false perception. It can't cover up the reality of who you are. The first rule of branding is to start with a quality product. In creating a personal brand, you are the product and you must be able to deliver. Let's say that you are identified within your company as the person who always gets things done on time. That is your personal brand promise. Your customers are other employees. You must deliver on that promise in each and every interaction with your customers. If you fail to get a task accomplished on time for a colleague, you have broken your brand promise. You have chipped away at your customer's perception of your value. You can't be late. Not even once. Your personal brand is unforgiving. That's why your brand must be developed based upon reality.

Although you can reflect upon the essence of who you are and see the positive qualities that make you a good person, most people are not fortunate enough to see your inner beauty and greatness. Instead, they make decisions based upon what they see, hear, and feel when they interact with you. As such, you deserve to be positioned in the best light. If you are happy with yourself, then you should use personal branding to present your best qualities to the world. Every point of contact should be designed to help you make a positive impression on your customers.

An owner of a brand controls its reputation by managing all the points where the audience comes in contact with the brand. The starting point for managing these contact points is the brand's strategy—knowing what kind of reputation he wants the brand to have in the minds of its audience. What reputation do you want to hold in the hearts and minds of your audience? What reputation will give you the greatest advantage over your competition?

Businesses employ entire teams of marketing professionals to help position them. What resources do you have? How can you take on the competition without a wealth of resources? The good news is that you can be as effective as the big guys with the resources that you currently have. You can develop a very effective personal brand, develop a personal communications strategy, and conceive and execute creative tactics that will effectively position you exactly as your customers should see you.

YOUR PERSONAL BRANDING CHALLENGE

As you develop your personal brand, your challenge is to make sure you are at the top of the list in the minds of your customers. In this context, the term "customers" refers to anyone who has a choice for a product or service that you provide. The product could be a tangible item, a day's work, friendship, or a warm meal. If they have a choice and there is mutual benefit in the relationship, consider them customers.

Branding is not about you; it's entirely about your customers. The experience they have when they interact with you—whether via e-mail, the telephone, or in person—forms an impression and creates an expectation in their mind. You want that interaction to be a positive one that leads to future interactions and referrals.

Establishing a personal brand strategy keeps the needs and the desires of your customers in the forefront of your mind. It helps you remain focused on that which is important to a group of people who can have a huge impact on your future—your customers.

Your goal in personal branding is to get your target market to see you as the preferred choice. You can do this by articulating what you do differently from everyone else and why that difference is better. However, making the promise—articulating the difference—is only half of the bargain. You must deliver on that promise each and every time. In other words, don't write checks you can't cash.

The personal branding process isn't about overwhelming advertisements, media plans, fancy logos, and catchy jingles. As you devise a specific strategy for creating a personal brand, you can expect to:

- Differentiate yourself from your competition
- Position your focused message to your target customers
- Develop consistent, focused marketing efforts
- Project credibility
- Strike an emotional chord
- Create strong loyalty

There are five rules to remember as you begin the process of developing your personal brand. They are:

You are what you are. Popeye would be proud. Anytime you represent yourself to be something that you are not, you run the risk of losing a customer forever. You have great qualities that can help position you as different and valuable. Those qualities must be your own. You must be honest with your customers—and with yourself.

Consistency is critical. Regardless of the business you are in, your customers must be able to count on you. If you want to impress your boss, don't complete an assignment early one time—beat your deadline every time. Your boss will know that you are the go-to person if she must have a critical project completed on time.

There are no "do-overs." First impressions are critical. You can't take back something you said to a customer. Everything is on the record. You should be yourself, but always remember that your reputation takes a lifetime to build and just a few minutes to destroy. Follow the Golden Rule in every interaction: Do unto others as you would have them do unto you. No one ever truly wins an argument with a customer.

Clarity is a gift. Too many people use complex language in order to appear intelligent and just wind up confusing people. Often, complexity makes the speaker seem pompous and condescending. Keep every interaction and every point of contact clear and simple. Be transparent. Communicate simply and directly.

Show, don't tell. If you explain a concept to a customer, he may understand it intellectually. But, if you tell him a story, show him a picture, or perform a demonstration, he will make an emotional connection to the event, to the experience, and to you. The more of his senses you can involve, the stronger the impression you will make. The key word here is impression. Make an impact or you'll fade like a distant memory.

As you move forward to craft a strategy for your personal brand, everything you do should be in alignment with these rules. Likewise, once your strategy is complete and you begin to focus on creating tactics to implement it, your tactics should adhere to these five basic rules.

THE FIVE PS OF PERSONAL BRANDING

Critical to the success of your personal brand are five qualities that I call "The Five Ps of Personal Branding." They are patience, proof, passion, persistence, and perspective.

Patience

Building a strong, meaningful brand takes time. Branding is more than flash-in-the-pan hype. Brands build momentum, which, in turn, helps fuel the customers' perception of the brand.

The New York Yankees are a great example of a brand that has built tremendous momentum over time. During interviews, you will often hear players on opposing teams talk about the "Yankee Mystique." They describe it as a workman-like approach to the game of baseball, along with a knack for mastering the big moment. It is, undoubtedly, the 26 world championships and the legacy of Hall of Fame players that have fueled this perception.

Walter Cronkite is an example of a fantastic personal brand that developed over time. Trust and credibility were the hallmarks of his tenure in television news. The perception of those characteristics could only have been built through years of delivering on a brand promise to his clients—his audience.

Proof

Brands must grow from the inside out. A brand must be genuine and offer proof to its constituents that it is the real deal. Public relations, advertising, and promotions can help put the best face on just about any situation; however, the public will eventually uncover a disingenuous brand.

The Atkins Nutritional Approach is an example of a brand that did not live up to the promise it made to its constituents. In 1972, Dr. Robert Atkins developed a diet that was intended to provide an enjoyable way to lose and maintain one's ideal weight. The diet was built on the principle that low carbohydrate intake and high protein consumption would allow a person to lose weight and maintain a healthy physical condition while enjoying even high fat foods in significant quantities.

After its initial success in the early 1970s, the Atkins diet's popularity waned until the low-carb diet craze took hold in 2002. Within two years, however, that bubble burst and the flaws in the Atkins brand were exposed on two fronts. First, dieters reported that after initially losing a significant amount of weight, their weight loss would plateau. They also found that the eating plan was unsustainable in the long term—that virtually no one could live on fewer than 50 grams of carbohydrates per day for the rest of her life. When dieters resumed eating carbohydrates—even in small amounts for a few days—they rapidly regained the lost weight. Second, mainstream health care professionals took a very public stance that low-carbohydrate diets high in saturated fats could contribute to coronary heart disease and a variety of other health problems.

The diet's only credible advocate—Dr. Atkins—tragically passed away in 2003. After his death, even the company's legions of hired guns could not defend the Atkins brand from its detractors. After capitalizing on the low-carb fad by rolling out lines of food products and developing Atkins University, an online diet program, Atkins Nutritionals, Inc. finally faced the music. In July 2005, the company was forced to declare bankruptcy. It took over three decades, but the brand finally succumbed to its inability to provide consumers with proof of its efficacy.

Passion

Brands must make an emotional connection with consumers. They must inspire their customers to feel a certain way about their products. They cannot simply win over their customers' minds, but they must also win over their hearts.

There are many branding examples in the world of politics, but one of my favorites is the repeated refusal of the American public to support tax increases on the wealthy. It seems that every time a tax increase for the small percentage of the population that makes over $200,000 per year comes up for debate, the American public is against it. Less than two percent of the American population is fortunate enough to have an income that meets or exceeds this level, yet even a discussion of this topic rubs middle-class Americans the wrong way.

One reason that the majority of Americans do not support increased taxes on the wealthiest 2 percent of the population lies in the emotional nature of America as a brand. Our great country was founded upon the right to life, liberty, and the pursuit of happiness. It's that last one that really tugs at our heartstrings. We all believe that the pursuit of happiness includes the potential to become rich. We all have hope that we will one day be in the top 2 percent of wage earners. That aspiration is an emotional attachment to the brand of America. Punishing someone (taxing the rich more heavily) for benefiting from our country's brand promise just feels wrong.

Persistence

Persistence is valuable in a number of areas, but it is essential in branding. Patience combined with persistence moves a brand to its ideal state.

I have met a number of people who have leveraged persistence into personal brand-building success. One of the great stories of a successful brand is a company called The Briad Group. Brad Honigfeld (Briad's founder and president) was a restaurant and catering manager with Marriott who took a chance and struck out on his own with only the money in his retirement account. He worked hard and opened a Roy Rogers restaurant that quickly became successful. Brad loved the TGI Friday's brand and wanted to open TGI Friday's restaurants in his local area. At the time, he was virtually unknown in the restaurant franchise community so Carlson Company (TGI Friday's parent company) would not approve his franchisee application.

Through persistence and dogged determination, Brad eventually broke through the barrier of being unknown. He became known (and is still known) as someone who aggressively pursues success in all of his business ventures. Companies like Carlson, Hilton, Wendy's International, and Marriott routinely bet on Brad's personal brand because of his persistence.

The consistency and clarity of Brad's message over the years—"I will be successful no matter what it takes"—has helped reinforce his personal brand in the minds of his customers and his business partners time and again.

Perspective

Branding works as long as it is customer-focused. A company must always approach its brand from its customers' perspectives—both today and in the future. The road to failure is paved with companies who had perceptions that were different than those of their customers.

Amtrak is a perfect example of this aspect of branding. Once upon a time, the railroad was a great way to travel. It moved people from one place to another efficiently and safely while providing an enjoyable experience. Today, it is a joke. Railroads in the United States are a business in such disarray that a private company will not even take a chance operating one without the help of the federal government.

Amtrak has a great opportunity to provide fast, efficient service to travelers in the Northeastern United States. The trip from New York to Boston or New York to Washington, D.C., could be a better experience on a train than it is on a plane. It may take a little longer (although security delays and bad weather often make the timing comparable), but the process of getting to your destination without the anxiety of air travel could be worth it.

The problem is perception. Customers perceive Amtrak as transportation. They evaluate it based upon transportation standards. Considerations like safety, efficiency, reliability, and service are important to the customer. Amtrak perceives itself as a railroad. Even worse, it perceives itself as a railroad with no competition. Why invest in infrastructure if there is no one competing with you? Why hire better employees or spend money training them if there is no one to steal away your best? Amtrak's perception does not match that of its customers. Therefore, its brand positioning is all wrong and it hemorrhages money every year.

Don't fall into this trap. Make sure you always evaluate your brand from the perspective of your customers. If you are ever wondering what your customers are thinking about your brand—ask them.

THE PROCESS OF DISCOVERY

Building your personal brand starts with a process of discovery. You need to identify your target audience and competition, the ways in which you can differentiate yourself from your competition, how you are currently perceived, and the ways in which you can address both the rational and emotional components of what your brand offers.

Who Are Your Targets?

The target for your brand communications is the group of people who are most likely to respond positively to your message or offer. Considering the resources you have available, you must decide whom you can effectively reach. You need to understand them and how they purchase your services. You need to understand how they perceive you and how they perceive the problems that you can solve for them. You must also understand how they feel about you and how you deliver your services.

If you are working in a corporate environment, you may have several different types of customers. Certainly your boss is someone whose perception you want to influence. You also want to make an impression on any customers or clients who use your products and services. Finally, you need to make a positive impression on your peers and subordinates. Each of these groups has a perception that could be important to your career.

As an entrepreneur or small business owner, you may have one less target audience—the boss—with which you need to communicate. However, if your business has investors, they will replace the boss as one of your target audiences.

All of these audiences—your communications targets—are brand stakeholders. They all have an interest or a stake in the future of your business or career.

Who Is Your Competition?

When thinking of ways to position yourself, you need to review potential competition both in terms of direct competition—those who can provide the same products and services that you provide to your stakeholders—and indirect competition—those who compete with different products and services that are equally valuable to your target audience.

For example, let's say that you are an insurance salesperson. Having no life insurance—doing nothing—is an option for your customers. They can simply stash their money in a mattress and let their significant other know where the money is located in case of a catastrophic event. Because a savings account or mutual fund also provides the means to save for the future, they would also significantly compete with your insurance product. In essence, your competitive set consists of every alternative that your target audience may choose instead of your product, service, or idea.

If you are in an office and you are the only person in your role, that doesn't necessarily mean that you have no competition. When it comes time to hand out bonuses, you want to get the largest possible share of the pie. Let's say you are the head of distribution and both you and the accounting leader report to the same supervisor. The boss has a limited number of bonus dollars to allocate to those who directly report to him. Because you want to get the most money possible, you are in direct competition with the accounting leader. The employee who offers the higher perception of value to the boss will receive the greater bonus.

Which External Factors Affect Communication?

The environment in which you live and work has an effect on you. The message you try to convey may be distorted, redirected, or misinterpreted based upon external factors. It is your duty to assess the external environment and determine if these external factors will have a bearing upon your objective in positioning your own personal brand.

Let's say, for example, that you are requesting a raise from your boss. You have thoughtfully prepared your message and you have a solid plan for presenting your body of work in the best light. You feel confident that you have a clear point of differentiation between yourself and your competition. As you prepare to begin your positioning campaign, you learn that your company has reported disappointing financial results. You also learn that, in order for the company to stay in business, layoffs are imminent. Will this external factor (the company's financial state is external to your individual brand) have an impact on your ability to achieve your objective? You bet it will.

How Are You Different?

The next step is to differentiate yourself from your competition. It is not enough to be better—you also need to be different. You need to demonstrate that difference to your clients and prospects early and often.

There are many different ways to set yourself apart from your competition. The quickest and most effective way is to focus on a specific area or niche of an industry. The more specialized your services are, the more you'll stand out from the crowd, and the more demand there will be for your services.

A narrow and deep approach can work for virtually anyone in any business or industry. It even worked for a friend of mine who was a police officer in New York City for over 20 years. Let's call him Keith (not his real name).

When Keith was promoted to detective, he worked in the Narcotics division. After a few transfers and promotions, he found himself investigating crimes related to a few specific gangs in an undesirable neighborhood in New York City. Keith was able to solve key cases involving these gangs during his early years in Narcotics. He knew the gangs well and he began to learn more about where the drugs they sold originated. Keith learned bits and pieces of information and then he would fit it all together like a puzzle. He discovered that all of the gangs seemed to be related. Keith eventually realized that they all rolled up to the same leadership structure outside of the United States. This large criminal enterprise became well-known through the media coverage of their horrific crimes—and they were big business in both New York and Colombia.

Through the efforts of the NYPD, it became difficult for the gangs to sell drugs in New York City. This forced them to develop affiliations in other states. South Florida was one of the places where the gang imported and sold drugs. As the drug flow into

South Florida began to point more specifically to the same group that was once such a problem in New York, Keith was called upon to offer his insight. He was the person who best knew this particular crime syndicate. He had a narrow and deep focus.

As time passed, Keith developed an even deeper expertise in this criminal enterprise. He made several trips to Colombia to gain more knowledge. He learned about their reporting structure and their business enterprises, both inside the United States and beyond its borders. This knowledge served him well in fighting crime in New York, but he continued to be a resource for agencies outside of the state.

When Keith retired from the NYPD after 20 years of service, he went to work for the U.S. Drug Enforcement Agency. They found his expertise on the Colombian drug trade to be incredibly valuable. In a federal law enforcement role, he was able to gather intelligence in areas well beyond the confines of any single city. This earned him promotions, pay increases, and several awards. Keith made two entire careers out of his specialty. His narrow and deep focus enabled him to become the most sought-after expert in his field.

How Are You Perceived?

Before you can get to a point where you have a clear consistent plan for your personal brand positioning, you must understand how people perceive you in your current state. You cannot determine where you want to go until you thoroughly understand where you are.

Soliciting deeply personal feedback is one of the most difficult things you will attempt. It is human nature to act defensively or to disbelieve the feedback you get from your peers, subordinates, or customers. It is not natural to separate yourself emotionally from the way other people perceive you. You have made an emotional investment in your own future and you don't want to hear that others have an opinion that differs from your own point of view. Yet, you need to make certain that you understand the perception that others have of your personal brand in order to try to influence that perception in the future.

To help make this uncomfortable situation work effectively, view the perception as detached from the reality. To do this, you must first make an agreement with yourself that you are a good person. You must also accept the fact that people may view you differently then you view yourself—and the very purpose of this exercise is to help shape the perception that others have of you. Once you have reconciled this in your mind, you can move forward with the research that is necessary to determine the current state of your brand.

If you approach this task with an open mind, you will find that there are a number of clues that point to the perception that others have of you and your personal brand. More often than not, people are hesitant to give you direct feedback on how you are perceived. Most people—particularly friends—will feel that this type of feedback will harm your relationship with them. Customers are a different story. If you have customers who work with you directly, you will often find that they will provide you with direct feedback on how they perceive you.

If you find that you are having a difficult time soliciting feedback on your own behalf, there is a technique that often breaks down the barrier of discomfort that may exist. Interview your target on behalf of a hypothetical third party. Do not refer to yourself at all during the process.

Let's say that you are an accountant and you want to understand the perception of your clients to help position your brand and ultimately gain additional financial planning business. Essentially, you are looking to expand your practice beyond tax accounting and into a role as an investment advisor. You could call five of your tax clients (who you know use someone else to help with financial planning) and interview them over the phone. You should start by asking about the services you currently provide and attempt to get feedback directly. Then you should ask them questions about the criteria they use to establish a new relationship in financial planning. Ask them which qualities they find helpful in a financial advisor. Ask them what they like the most about this service and what they would like to see done more efficiently. In this case, you may not receive a great deal of direct feedback about your brand, but this information will be helpful in determining how you could position yourself to others in the future. You can take the answers you receive and extrapolate information about where you are now.

The primary objective for this process is to assess where you are and where you need to be in order to occupy the appropriate space in the mind of your target. You need to find out how you can appropriately position yourself to your customer.

How Can You Balance the Rational and Emotional Aspects of Your Offering?

Earlier chapters discussed the rational and emotional aspects of decision making. As you move forward in positioning your personal brand, you must also look at the rational and emotional aspects of this process. Ultimately, you are asking your target audience to make a decision to choose you.

If everyone made decisions or developed perceptions based upon the rational aspects of a product or service, then brands would only need to communicate the functional properties they possess. In reality, the emotional aspect of a decision often trumps all of the rational features and benefits associated with a product or service.

As you develop your personal brand, you must make certain that you have addressed both the rational and the emotional components of your offering. After all, you can never be certain which aspect will provide your target with a more compelling motivation to work with you.

You must keep the rational and emotional aspects of your brand in balance. Imagine them on a scale with the rational components—attributes and benefits—on one side and the emotional components—values and personality—on the other. Your goal is to strike equilibrium in your offering to your target audience.

On the rational side, you must decide what attributes you have to offer as a brand. In other words, how would you describe yourself from a functional perspective? What can you do? What skills and knowledge do you have? What are your talents? You also need to look at the benefits of working with you. What does someone who works with you get? How do you make his life better? What problem do you solve?

On the emotional side, you must first look at the values you possess. How will working with you make your client feel? What makes you a good person or business partner? Finally, you should look at personality. What is your personality and how will it be conveyed to your client? What makes you who you are? Are you deeply intellectual? Are you a calming influence? The key is to realize that you're striving for a complete package. You may know everything about everything, but if that guy sitting across the table from you doesn't like you for some reason, or feels your personality isn't a good fit for whatever he's selling, then your expertise is damaged by your lack of charisma or personality.

THE MEDIUM IS THE MESSAGE

Once you have decided what impression you want to make on your target audience, you need to decide how to convey that impression to your stakeholders. Methods of getting the word out are called brand distribution channels.

The approach to distributing a personal brand differs slightly from the approach used by a large company. For example, as an individual, you can take more risk than a large company can. You don't need to go through a drawn-out approval process to position your personal brand. In most cases, the number of points of contact between your personal brand and your constituents are far fewer than the number of points of contact between a company and its customers. This makes it easier for you to fulfill the promise made by your personal brand.

These differences, combined with the fewer resources you have as an individual, mean that your approach to brand distribution is significantly different from that of a large company. The enormous resources available to a big business allow it to saturate all brand channels simultaneously. This may or may not be an effective brand strategy. In most cases, choosing brand channels carefully and strategically makes more sense than a saturation approach. In all cases, each point of contact must have the ability to integrate with the other points of contact. In short, the approach for a personal brand could work (and has worked) for large companies, but the approach for a large company is rarely practical or cost effective for a personal branding campaign.

The following illustration shows the approach for an individual seeking to establish a personal brand presence:

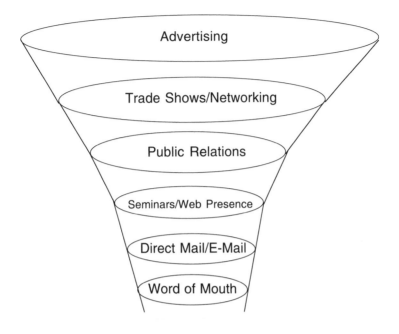

As you can see from the illustration, all of the work you do in creating a brand for yourself leads to creating an environment where people recommend you, your products, and your services. Word of mouth is everything in personal brand distribution. To ensure the growth and development of your personal brand, people must talk about you in a favorable way. Generating and maintaining positive word of mouth is the hand-to-hand combat of brand development. Although large companies often neglect this aspect of marketing, the next chapter focuses on it extensively. Positive word of mouth—advocacy—is your goal in establishing your personal brand.

The funnel also illustrates the nature of each distribution channel. Following is an outline of the primary channels and their potential use in positioning your personal brand:

Advertising

Advertising—whether in print or broadcast media, the Internet, or on signage—works to establish awareness for a brand.

Although Intrepreneurs probably won't utilize advertising, Entrepreneurs may find advertising to be an opportunity to make an impression in a clear, concise way. It is also efficient and effective in reaching large audiences, and its message can be easily controlled and customized to your target audience. In addition, advertising lends itself to measurability; you can use metrics to see if you have positioned your brand to reach your target audience. In some cases, such as with promotional advertising, it will help drive traffic to you or your business. Stimulating curiosity about you or what you have to offer is often the desired outcome of an advertising campaign.

The primary drawback of advertising is that it is expensive to implement and maintain. In addition, you have to overcome the conditioning that leads people to ignore traditional advertisements. Further, advertising is a one-way communication that offers no interaction with your target audience.

Trade Shows

The primary purpose of participating in a trade show is to help increase your exposure to the target audience in your industry or in a feeder industry—an industry that provides you with clients. If you are an Entrepreneur, you may decide to become a vendor and display your products in a booth in order to reach many people in a short period of time. If you are an Intrepreneur, you will want to visit with company representatives at a trade show because they may be good prospective employers. Trade shows are also great places to scout out the competition and pick up the best practices in your field.

The downside of exhibiting in a trade show is the expense—for everything from booth rental and shipping to travel and overnight accommodations. In addition, attendees have a low incidence of recall of specific people, products, or services from trade shows because they see so many of them.

Networking

The purpose of networking—whether by attending your local Chamber of Commerce events, volunteering at charitable functions, or joining a fraternal organization—is to make contacts that may lead to future business. Networking can help Entrepreneurs develop contacts with vendors who may supply your business with necessary goods or services. The Intrepreneur will benefit from networking within her industry because it helps her understand the value of her services and allows her to keep her eyes open for new and exciting opportunities. Both groups can benefit from the friendships that form at networking events and from the news and information that is typically available before it hits the mainstream media or trade press. In addition, you can quickly establish your expertise within your local community.

The downside to networking is that it is time intensive and that you don't see immediate results. Furthermore, the local nature of networking can constrict your sphere of influence.

Public Relations

Public relations opportunities—such as being interviewed by the broadcast or print media, or being tapped for a corporate newsletter article that establishes you as the go-to person for information on a specific topic—can be used to enhance your image, maintain or develop goodwill with your community, and reinforce your credibility as an expert in your field. Because of the implied third-party endorsement of a publication or television show, you can gain credibility. Compared with other communication channels, public relations opportunities are usually inexpensive. They also allow you to reach your target audience through programming and editorial choices. Public relations can exist within an organization or external to an organization, so Entrepreneurs and Intrepreneurs can both benefit from enhanced public relations efforts.

The primary drawback of public relations opportunities is that you have little control over the content of your message. There is always the possibility that you will be misquoted or that what you say may be taken out of context. Like advertising, public relations provides one-way communication to your target audience, but, unlike advertising, it is difficult to measure. Finally, if your intent is to make a national or international splash, you may need to engage the services of a public relations expert, which can be very expensive.

Seminars

The primary purpose of a seminar is to educate people on the intricacies of your industry and your role in that industry. You can increase your value to your target audience by demonstrating a new, unreleased product or by inviting the media to preview and discuss an embargoed report. As you educate your audience, you are also increasing your credibility. Plus, you can create a lasting impression on the people who attend, as well as those who can't make it. No one likes to miss a special event.

Intrepreneurs can conduct internal seminars to educate colleagues on an area in which they are experts. I know a man who increased his exposure within his organization by conducting CPR classes (he was a Red Cross volunteer in his free time). The president of the company attended and was certified by my friend, who is now on a first name basis with the company president.

If you're not comfortable in a public speaking role, this tactic may not be beneficial for you. In order to succeed in increasing your credibility and brand status, you need to enjoy being the center of attention. Unless you can place yourself in a position to be invited to give a presentation, producing and hosting your own seminar can be both expensive and time consuming.

Web Presence

For both Entrepreneurs and Intrepreneurs, a Web site and a regularly updated Weblog (blog) can be a tremendous benefit in helping you establish your personal brand. A Web site is available 24–7–365 and can provide a plethora of information about you that can help enhance your credibility. Newspaper clippings can live on forever on your site, as can your educational achievements, your biography, and your résumé.

A good blog can be a forum for you to comment on the events of the day, as well as to offer free advice or tips that help position you as an expert. This will also serve to increase your credibility while drawing the attention of people who may be searching for information on topics that you have written about.

This distribution channel gives you the advantage of being able to include marketing collateral and being able to build word of mouth through visitors referring your site to their friends and colleagues. In addition, because the user chooses what he wants to see and when he wants to see it, interactivity is high. If you include a live chat feature or e-mail link, you can create two-way communication with your target audience.

The primary drawback to creating and maintaining a Web site or blog is the time it takes to create enough new content to keep visitors coming back. It can also take time to build up traffic to your site or blog, which can be initially discouraging.

Direct Mail and E-mail

The purpose of direct mail and e-mail is to reach a highly targeted audience with a specific message. Both mediums have the ability to provide a personal touch to a mass mailing, and both can increase your credibility by virtue of the fact that your recipients will come to view you as an expert if you send them information that says you're an expert. Regular mailings can effectively keep your name in front of prospective customers over the course of months or even years.

The major downside to direct mail is that it is expensive to produce quality material and mail it to your target audience. Even though e-mail is inexpensive to send, it is time-intensive to create and maintain mailing lists. In addition, both direct mail and e-mail blasts need to set the right tone and convey useful information in order for your target audience to be receptive to your message and read your content.

Although each of these brand distribution channels can be an effective means of creating a favorable impression for your personal brand, they all funnel down into word of mouth. What you really want are advocates—people who tell other people about your wonderful products or services.

Chapter Eight

GENERATE BUZZ

What's the buzz about your personal brand? When there's a lull in conversation, do people fill it by talking about the wonders of your product, or do you feel like a kid with a lemonade stand on a busy corner, watching the cars speed by? During powerbroker conversations, does your name come up as a superachiever, or are you the wallflower at the hottest cocktail party in town?

The effort you have put into creating Career Intensity is wasted if people don't notice the career you have built. Whether you're an Entrepreneur or an Intrepreneur, you need to create advocates—people who tell others about the positive aspects of your products and services and who encourage others to give you a try or to use you again.

When you create awareness—through word of mouth—of the value you provide, you're positioning your personal brand. This positive word of mouth becomes buzz, which you can then convert into advancement opportunities.

You don't have millions of dollars to spend creating recognition for your personal brand and establishing the credibility and authority you need to compete with the dominant players in your market. Even if you did have the resources to deploy in expensive and time-consuming brand distribution channels, the best outcome you could generate would be to have large groups of your customers talk about you and the products and services you provide. This word of mouth would promote your brand and increase its recognition. This grassroots movement would be more effective than buying ad time during the Super Bowl.

Your own experience proves the point. Let's say that you're in the market for a new car, and you watch a commercial that airs during the Super Bowl. The commercial may catch your attention and may even entertain you. Beyond that, it only demonstrates that the company has the financial resources to advertise in an expensive venue. You would need to gather additional information before purchasing the car. Instead, imagine that your friend brings up the reliability of her new car during a casual conversation. Most likely, you pay close attention and use what she says to inform your decision. More often than not, the opinions of your friends and family are more valuable to you than any information conveyed through an advertisement. More products are sold over the dinner table or on the golf course than are ever sold through ads in the *New York Times* and on television.

Surely, large companies must have an advantage over the sole proprietor when it comes to creating advocates since they can deploy significant resources at their disposal to effectively and quickly spread the word about their product. This is absolutely not the case. Even though the resources of a large corporation may allow it to increase its brand recognition, they do nothing to help the company stimulate additional positive word of mouth. In fact, most major corporations do not know how to harness the awesome power of consumer advocacy.

Likewise, the Intrepreneur can increase his personal brand recognition within his company and generate and leverage positive word of mouth to help influence the perception people have of him. In fact, the people who are the most respected in many companies are often those who have the best reputations. This perception is created almost exclusively through word of mouth within their firms. In many professional service firms (law firms, accounting firms, and consultancies), performance criteria is only a partial determinant of career advancement. In those cases, partners or senior level managers are elected to their positions. If you are employed in one of these organizations, word of mouth has a huge impact on your future.

Once you have a message that is compelling, you need to find a way to get people to spread that message. Many people subscribe to the philosophy that providing a good product is enough to get people to talk about it. This simply is not true. In the case of your personal brand, simply doing a good job will not get you noticed. Perfect performance is not good enough to make your career aspirations a reality. You must activate the social networks and the expert networks that can generate buzz and help spread your message.

There is a systematized way to activate these networks and utilize them to serve your needs. In essence, you need to understand how the networks function—who talks, why they talk, and how you can plug into this powerful force.

WHO'S TALKING NOW?

Network architecture is a technical name for groups of people that talk to one another and spread messages. It is your goal to plug into this network to disseminate your message. In order to connect, you must first understand the individuals that are critical to helping generate buzz about your product or service. Some people—whom I call "repeaters"—are more prone than others to sharing information. Although it's true that each one of us shares information with others all the time, the average person may share a story or anecdote with two or three people. A repeater will share a story with 100 or more people. Another way to view this concept is to say that the repeater will increase the exposure of a story exponentially.

As an example, let's say I have two friends who both fly on Jet Blue, and they both have a great experience. My friend Paul tells his friends and his family that he enjoyed his experience, and he says that he will definitely fly with them again. He will recommend Jet Blue to people who ask him about flying to Ft. Lauderdale. My friend Darcy is a repeater. She tells everyone in her family about the experience of flying on Jet Blue—down to the most finite detail. She talks about being able to watch *Oprah* while the plane was on its way to Ft. Lauderdale. She remarks that the staff was friendly and helpful, both at the gate and on the plane. She tells this story in vivid detail, over and over again, to about 100 people during the course of a year. She will tell this story unsolicited. This story comes up when she talks about great customer service, innovation, experiences when traveling, and so forth.

Even though both Paul and Darcy will repeat their experiences to friends, Darcy will share the story with more people. She will also provide more detail about the experience, which will leave an indelible impression in people's minds. In addition, Darcy will tell the story unsolicited. She will share her experience on Jet Blue regardless of the topic of conversation. Darcy will also incorporate feedback from others into her story as time goes on. Paul will only share his experience when the topic is airline transportation and, even then, he may wait for someone to ask his opinion. It is both the quality of Darcy's interactions and the quantity of her links to other people that classify her as a repeater.

Everyone would love to have an army of repeaters (like my friend Darcy) helping spread the word about the value they provide. There are four things that make a repeater valuable to you in positioning your personal brand:

- She will share her experiences broadly throughout the community. If a regular user tells others his story five times in the course of a year, a repeater will tell the story over 100 times.
- She will tell a vivid story with detail that will make a lasting impression on her listener.
- She will initiate conversations about you, your product, or your service.
- Her conversations about you will be interactive, and she may add the feedback of others to the story when she tells it the next time.

Another type of individual—whom I call a "booster"—can be instrumental in creating word of mouth momentum. A booster is someone who not only has numerous two-way links, like a repeater, but who also has a platform that allows him to address mass quantities of people who take him seriously. He boosts the recognition of your brand or message by the sheer volume of people that listen to him and the credibility he holds with his audience. These boosters amplify your message in both volume and stature. Members of the press, celebrities, Wall Street analysts, church pastors, and sports figures often enjoy this type of status. Even though he is just one individual, the booster has the ability to create tremendous buzz just by discussing a person, product, or service.

Don Imus is a great example of a booster. His morning radio show is syndicated throughout the United States and is simulcast all over the world on cable and satellite television. If he talks about a book or a book's author, hundreds of thousands of people want additional information about the book, the author, and the topic. One appearance on his show can create tremendous buzz.

WHERE ARE THEY TALKING?

Repeaters and boosters operate in informal communications networks known as communities. There are two types of communities that are important to you in establishing the presence of your personal brand: communities that have specific content relevant to you, your products, or your services, and social communities that have groups of potential customers. The informal nature of each of these networks creates the fabric of today's society.

Repeaters in content-based communities are often viewed as experts, opinion leaders, or thought leaders. They have credibility within the community because of their depth of knowledge of the subject matter. Social communities are driven by charismatic individuals who network with others and form individual relationships with large groups of people. Repeaters in these communities derive their credibility from their social status and in the volume of people they know.

There may be overlap between these two communities. Your work environment may contain both. People who have significant credibility and are repeaters in one community may not have a special status in another. Although I would definitely ask my information technology expert at work which computer I should buy for my sister as a gift, I would not ask him to coordinate an office party. He is known in our office for his expertise in technology, but other colleagues are known for hosting fun parties. Your goal in personal marketing is to generate positive buzz through these networks to help create demand for the services you have to offer.

WHY ARE THEY TALKING?

People talk about products and services for a number of reasons. Understanding why people talk is necessary in order to influence them to serve as advocates for your products and services.

People exchange information because it is instinctive. Sharing information is a survival mechanism that is as natural as breathing. Animals that live in groups in the wild share information to help other members of the herd avoid danger and find food. When we find a product or a service that is harmful, we feel an instinctive need to share that information with others. Think of it as the caveman's legacy to us.

To observe this instinctive behavior firsthand, simply hang around the breakroom of any office. Aside from the usual gripes that you may encounter, you will always hear tales of company gossip. These stories are never short on detail and everyone listens to them, regardless of the credibility of the person who is sharing them. They listen because they have been programmed to do so. More often than not, and again with a lack of regard for the credibility of the source, they will repeat the same story they just heard. They may preface their comments by saying, "I'm not sure if this is true," but they talk about it nonetheless.

People also exchange information to connect with one another. Gossip developed out of this need to be connected. In most cases, talking about a third party is neutral common ground for two individuals. They can exchange information in a verbal dance as a means of social interaction. Again, this comes from our ancestors. In colonial times, when one person visited another person's home, they would bring a gift as a token of appreciation for having been received in the home of another. Today, conveying the latest scoop is a way of presenting a gift to colleagues who have received them in their workspace. It is also a way to segue into a necessary topic of conversation and, sometimes, is simply a way to kill time.

An exchange of information—particularly about products and services—also takes place when a person wants to demonstrate her status or standing in society. When she says, "Everyone knows that I get a new mobile phone when the latest model comes out" or "I love the level of service I get from my Mercedes dealer," she wants the other person to know that she has achieved the status associated with the product or service she has mentioned. Her motivation for name-dropping may be simply to show her social status, or it could be borne in insecurity. She may truly be unhappy with her social standing and may want to appear to be something that she is not. In either case, a good portion of the time, status is the reason individuals talk about people, products, and services.

Many people talk to one another out of a need to feel that there is order to the world or society in which we live. Every day we see things that we do not understand. We hear things that do not make sense to us. We need some type of validation. We need to know that, if what we have seen, heard, or felt are true, we are not alone. Some people refer to this process as a sanity check.

The sanity check has a close cousin called the reality check—when someone discusses other people, products, or services to ascertain that what he has experienced is true. He doesn't really think he's crazy; he just thinks that he may have received atypical service. He wants to know that his expectation for service, or that his reaction to his perception of poor service, is reasonable.

Because most people hate risk, especially when it is related to business or financial situations, they communicate with others to help mitigate risks or to increase their comfort levels in relation to risks they've taken. For example, I was recently forced to switch dentists due to relocation. Looking for a dentist whose services my insurance covers is a good first step, but beyond that, how do I select someone who will have free license to cause great pain and wave sharp objects in my face? Because I want to be certain that my new dentist is trustworthy, I will ask friends to recommend a dentist who they use and like.

In other cases, people speak with others to help relieve their own tension. In some cases, they are angry and need to vent. In others, they have fears that they need to alleviate. They want others to help them feel as though they are making sense. They are trying to rationalize their fears or feelings of inadequacy.

Many people talk about people, products, or services because they are uncomfortable with silence. The next time you are in a one-on-one conversation with someone, do not attempt to fill an awkward silence. If there is a lull in the conversation, just let the deafening quiet hang in the air. See if the other person says something unusual or provocative simply because they need to fill the silence. She may feel that saying something, anything, is better than that nasty silence. To break the silence, many times she will talk about someone who is not present or a neutral topic.

The challenge associated with these types of conversations is that it is far easier to talk about negative information than it is to speak about positive information. Negative information is just more newsworthy and seems to flow easier. In fact, as a society, we've been conditioned to spread negative news more readily than good news.

The media focuses 90 percent of its attention on shockingly horrible stories because they grab our attention. Most of the time, you take your car to the mechanic only when something is wrong with it. You stop smoking, drinking, or overeating only when you are faced with negative consequences. Your spouse does 100 things right every day, but the minute your significant other forgets something that causes you a minor inconvenience, you instantly condemn him. Moreover, you probably talk about all of the negative occurrences in your life.

Your challenge is to position your personal brand in a manner that allows it to replace the negative information that dominates most conversations.

WORKING COMMUNITIES BY TWEAKING REPEATERS

Creating advocates through word of mouth is the hand-to-hand combat of personal marketing. It is a true grass roots effort. At first, it appears that a personal marketer's best course of action is to connect with as many boosters as possible and hope the message filters down to the repeaters and spreads from there. Although this is ideal, boosters tend to be difficult to reach, even with an expert media relations team.

A more effective course of action is to reach out at the grass-roots level to as many repeaters as possible. This process creates a groundswell that will eventually give the boosters valuable information to include in reports to their throngs of constituents. Boosters are often hesitant to risk their reputation and status without the sense that there is substantial support for the brand in question.

A good example is Girard, who was the lead baker in a small bakery in Nashua, New Hampshire. At the age of 32, he decided he wanted to go out on his own. His family members had always complemented him on the unique taste of his peanut butter-almond cookies. He had developed this recipe when he was in high school, but had never made these cookies for public consumption.

Girard opened a small bakery in Manchester, New Hampshire, and the cookies were his signature item. His bakery was a full-service shop—offering an assortment of cakes, breads, and all kinds of pastries—but it was Girard's cookies that helped get the word out about his new bakery.

On numerous occasions, Girard invited reporters from the local newspapers and television and radio stations to taste "the best cookies in town." Unfortunately, Girard's media relations campaign was an abysmal failure. He tried everything—including sending cookies to the local media outlets—but never got the coverage he was seeking.

Finally, near the end of his first year in business, Girard's bakery received some acclaim from one of the local restaurant critics (who, in the community of Manchester, certainly fit the definition of a booster). One of the local schools had a bake sale and a rival bakery had donated cookies to the cause. Girard was on vacation and his bakery was closed when the event took place. Since the cookies were donated, the school simply added the name of the bakery to a donors' list, but did not label the cookies. Those who attended the bake sale believed that they were purchasing Girard's cookies because the look and texture was similar.

When he returned from vacation, Girard received visits from several customers who complained about the taste of the cookies he donated to the bake sale. Their biggest complaint was that the cookies were "missing something." Girard responded in a most unusual way. He explained that he did not donate to the bake sale because he was on vacation. He told each customer who complained about the taste of his competitor's cookies that he wished he could have been there to meet their expectations. He then gave them each a free box of cookies. Girard handed out over 150 boxes of cookies in a week, and the word spread around town that this was a baker who cared about his customers.

Gradually, the cookie story grew. One of the versions of the story compared Girard to Nordstrom department store. Nordstrom once gave store credit to a man that returned snow tires—and Nordstrom didn't even sell snow tires. Soon, people were bringing in cookies from all over town to "trade in" for Girard's cookies. Eventually, this word of mouth became so powerful that it caught the attention of the local media. At that point, the local television station sent their restaurant critic to taste the cookies—which he found to be outstanding. For months afterward, Girard sold thousands of cookies each week. People were coming from as far south as Boston to buy his cookies. The repeaters had given him the credibility necessary to tap into a major booster.

Girard's story illustrates the value of directing your efforts toward repeaters in order to create buzz and gain momentum. But, how do you get these conversations started?

Pulling to Get the Word Out

By and large, creating buzz is about interacting individuals talking about you, your products, or your services. Even though it is intuitive to believe that getting the word out should start with mass media via an advertising campaign or an extensive public relations effort, this requires time and money. Your personal brand lends itself very easily to being spread from one person to another.

Saturating the brand marketing channels is a push strategy. In essence, you are thrusting yourself upon the media and the world and you are hoping that boosters pick up your message and carry it through the repeaters down to the grassroots individuals. It is far more effective to reach out to the grassroots level first and spread upward to the repeaters and up further to the boosters. In fact, people at the grassroots level may become repeaters in certain social communities or industries. Unfortunately, the first time you communicate your message, you have no way of knowing who the repeaters are.

Most experts agree that in any given community—either social or expert—about 10 to 15 percent of the population will spread information exponentially as repeaters. If you can come up with the right message and inject it directly into the community at the grassroots level, you stand a good chance of pulling your message through the repeaters to the boosters—essentially pulling it up the communications funnel instead of pushing it down. This, in turn, will magnify your message and help it reach new communities.

Many creative people with a few resources and a lot of ingenuity use a combination push-pull strategy. In business, this is referred to as integrated marketing communications. Messages are crafted at each level of the brand distribution chain and work hand in hand with one another. An ad campaign may create some interest on the part of news outlets because it is controversial, or a seminar may generate interest among the trade press because it is sold out or because it is an exclusive, invitation-only event. All the while, the grassroots members of the community are being seeded with messages related to the topic of the seminar or the ad campaign. Pull and push—all the way up and down the brand distribution funnel.

Ultimately, the message you create about your personal brand must lend itself well to both pushing and pulling. Even if you have zero resources to allocate to advertising, tradeshows, or seminars, your message needs to be newsworthy—or at least worth talking about in the breakroom or at the water cooler.

There are three characteristics of a brand that help its message travel through the grassroots to repeaters and up to boosters: passion or energy, credibility, and durability.

Passion and Energy

Because you're developing a personal brand, you must be passionate about your product or service. Intrepreneurs should enthusiastically volunteer for high-profile assignments that no one else wants. Take jobs that will result in high exposure. Entrepreneurs will demonstrate their passion and energy when they take on challenging tasks and win.

Sometimes, just enthusiastically surviving a challenging assignment is enough to raise your standing in the eyes of others. Attorney Mark Geragos is a great example of this phenomenon. Although Mr. Geragos has a successful and distinguished career as a defense attorney, two cases that he lost gave him the most exposure and, many would say, credibility because he was brave enough to take them on in the first place. Geragos defended Winona Ryder in her shoplifting case and Scott Peterson in his murder trial. Both of these cases were losses, but they showed that Geragos was not afraid of a tough challenge. In both cases, the evidence was firmly stacked against his client. The energy he brought to these tough cases made many people sit up and take notice. Undoubtedly, other high-profile people with stronger cases will not hesitate to call him because they know that he can handle this type of situation.

Credibility

Your personal credibility can also help to pull your message through a community. Let's say you go to your doctor—your regular physician—complaining of pain in your knee. She examines you and tells you that you need to see a specialist. Assuming that your insurance will cover a visit to any doctor, how do you determine which specialist to see? Do you go to the Yellow Pages and look up "knee doctors" or "orthopedic surgeons"? Not likely. In most cases, you ask your general practitioner for a referral to a specialist because your experience with her has led you to believe she has credibility and that you can trust her judgment. Her credibility is then transferred to the specialist to whom she refers you.

Personal credibility can influence product choices as well as choices for services. For example, there is very little difference between a store brand of toothpaste and brand-name toothpaste. When you go to your dentist's office for a cleaning, he may give you a complimentary toothbrush along with a tube of toothpaste. If your dentist gives you a certain brand of toothpaste, you may believe he thinks it is superior to other brands. In other words, his credibility transfers to the brand of toothpaste he gives his patients.

Durability

There are really two elements to the durability of a brand: the need to stand the test of time and the need to survive distraction. Both of these elements require a strong brand foundation, as well as the ability of the brand to make necessary adjustments over the course of time.

The New York Stock Exchange is a prime example of surviving distraction. This pillar of the economic system for the most advanced economy in the world was shaken to its core by terrorist attacks on September 11, 2001. Yet, in less than a week, the Exchange was up and running with sufficient redundant systems that inspired confidence around the world.

Two years after that event, the institution was again rocked, but this time by controversy involving executive compensation. Despite the distraction of bad press, tragedy, and controversy, this institution has persevered and remains the cornerstone of the capitalist economic system.

The ability to stand the test of time—durability—is the hallmark of a great brand. The phenomenal entertainer Cher is a great example of this quality. Her brand is as strong today as it was in the 1960s when she hit the stage with her then-husband Sonny Bono.

In the '60s and '70s, Cher was best known as a television and recording star. In the '80s and '90s, Cher became a respected film actress. Today, Cher has evolved into one of the most popular recording artists in the dance-music genre while continuing to make movies. Her personal brand has survived the distraction of the fads of the past four decades. Cher fulfills the promise of her personal brand by being a world-class entertainer in spite of the changing faces of the entertainment industry.

The power of passion and energy, durability, and credibility is that they are shared through interactivity. Unlike many brand marketing channels, the recipient of the information has the ability to ask questions and interact with the advocate. This is where the true perception of passion and energy, credibility, and durability leave a lasting impression.

Seeding the Grassroots

To accomplish the penetration you need to generate word of mouth at the grassroots level, you must first understand the community where you will find the audience that is most receptive to your message. What is the common factor for the particular community that you want to penetrate? Do the members of your target audience live or work in the same area? Do they regularly travel through the same area? Is the community based upon a body of specific knowledge? It is critical to determine the factor that binds these individuals together as a community.

Observation is the most effective way of identifying the factor that binds a community. Let's say I am an Entrepreneur and I want to convey the message that I just opened a sporting goods store. One of my likely targets is a parent with children who play sports. In stimulating interest in my store, I have to identify the community I should target. First, I would look to see what common elements this group would share. Town-based athletic leagues jump to the forefront of my mind. Each league is its own community. If I wanted to communicate to soccer moms, I could approach the league organizers—boosters—and communicate through them. Although they might be initially hesitant to endorse me, I could at least spark their interest. Next, I could attend local games, talk to some moms directly, and hand out flyers and offer discounts specific to that particular town's league. I could then repeat this process in each town within a 30-mile radius of my store.

The process of finding the common thread in the community is critical to the success of the message. More often than not, groups of potential communications targets go unnoticed. When I was a youngster, my family and I lived in Binghamton, New York, for two years. Binghamton is a city about four hours north of New York City. That area of New York is very cold—during the winter, it's not uncommon for the temperature to remain below freezing for weeks at a time—and receives significant snowfall every year.

Most of the schools in the Binghamton area allow children to play outside during lunch breaks as long as the wind chill does not push the temperature below zero. Parents obviously want to keep their children safe and healthy, but they want them to enjoy the winter wonderland that Binghamton becomes during the winter. (Did I mention that the area averages 83 inches of snow each year?)

When we first moved to the area, we noticed that all of the kids wore snowmobile suits to school. Since we were new in town, we did not know where to get these outfits. We visited several sporting goods stores, but they did not have what we needed. Finally, we found a ski shop with attractive and durable snowmobile suits that would last through the winter season. The next year, we needed to complete the same process because kids outgrow these one-piece overalls during the course of a season. In discussing the need to buy snowmobile suits with neighbors, my parents found out that the ski shops sold out of kids' sizes by November 1 each year.

A smart ski shop owner could have mounted a clever word of mouth campaign in September that his store had a good selection of snowmobile suits. He could have easily targeted moms of school-age children. A campaign in September would have allowed him to place two orders and sell twice as many snowmobile suits before the first snowfall. This never happened because none of the ski shops viewed parents of school-age children as an audience for their message. Word of mouth would spread through the parents as to which shops had good selections and when snowmobile suits were in stock. The ski shops lost out on the ability to control the information because they did not know what the community was saying about them.

Once you identify the community that is talking about your brand, you need to understand who in the community is talking. In the case of the ski shop story, it was the parents who picked up their kids at school every day. There was a 15-minute window of opportunity where the moms all stood around talking while they waited for the dismissal bell to ring. If the topics were compelling, sometimes the conversation extended beyond the pickup time. The repeater in this community was a woman who had five children. Taking care of her kids—who ranged in age from 4 to 12—was a full-time job, and one that she took very seriously. Since she had a kid in or just passing each grade in elementary school, she was a valuable resource for all of the moms. If she endorsed a person, a product, or a service, everyone knew about it. She was a powerful figure. A ski shop that could have won her endorsement would have had the opportunity to communicate with everyone in my elementary school.

How do you identify who is talking about you? Ask your customers. Informally asking around gives you solid clues as to where your communities of customers may lie. It will also help you identify valuable repeaters that you can tap to help spread the word about your personal brand, your products, and your services.

NUMBERS TELL BUT STORIES SELL

Throughout the ages, virtually every society has valued its storytellers. Ancient civilizations would rely on the village elders to tell stories to the young children in order to pass along the community's history. Stories were also used to train the youngsters for hunting and to face the challenges in the wild.

Today, we continue to place a premium on people who have the ability to tell a story. Television and motion picture actors, producers, and directors are highly sought after and regarded. Comedians and authors of novels are revered as extraordinarily gifted. Each is valued because each can influence the way you feel. When you go to the movies, you want to be thrilled, confused, or scared—without it having an impact on your life. When you see a comedy show, you want to laugh at someone else or at his misfortune. Like all of us, you love to experience emotions in a vicarious state. A good story makes you feel a certain way without the negative side effects.

In the consulting business, we often say that numbers tell, but stories sell. A client is more likely to believe a compelling story than he will believe cold, hard facts that are placed before him. Stories about others are successful because they allow the listener to put himself in the place of the subject of the story. He feels the actual emotion that the subject of the story feels. In his mind, he experiences the events of the story firsthand.

You need your customers to tell moving and emotional stories about you. You make your interaction with them into positive emotional experiences. They then need to feel compelled and overwhelmed enough to share those stories with other people. Spend some time thinking about the best interaction that someone has had with you. What is the one compelling story about you that elicits a positive reaction in others? Now imagine someone telling another person that story. What feelings do you think a total stranger would have if your best customer told that story?

In order to create that situation, you must become the type of person who others naturally talk about. One way to do that is to create a positive emotional response in your interaction with every customer. If two candidates are equally suited for a job—if all aspects of education, experience, and aptitude are equal—then the candidate who made the interviewer laugh will get the job every time. Sometimes the ability to evoke a positive emotion during an interview will even mask the shortcomings of a candidate. If you are the kind of person who makes others feel good about themselves, people will remember you favorably.

People also talk about other people or products that have their own form of natural publicity. Donald Trump, Paris Hilton, Madonna, and David Beckham are a few people who cannot even go shopping without creating a buzz. Everything they touch is a hot commodity because they create their own advertising. For some, it is the way they look. For others, it is their prowess in a field—such as television, business, or sports—that interests the public. The common denominator is that they all welcome the spotlight. They never pass up an opportunity to spend time advertising themselves. If you want to know how good they are, just ask them. Many people bristle at the thought of shameless self-promotion, but it is important to weigh the alternatives. If you promote yourself, people will talk about you. Some people will say positive things and others will say negative things—but they will all be talking. If you do not promote yourself, nobody will know who you are. Which is worse?

Another way to make it easy for people to talk about you is to leave them something to talk about after you are gone. This is a favorite tactic of mine at The Gallup Organization. Gallup authors have published some of the best-selling business books of the past decade. Every meeting I have with a prospective client includes a reference to material in one of our books. I would then—just by chance—leave that book in the reception area for someone to find. Nine times out of ten, this book was the subject of discussion that led to a follow-up phone call to my office.

Leaving something behind can be a simple as leaving a brochure or a business card, or sending a follow-up note a few days after a meeting. Anything you leave helps make you memorable and will lead to people telling stories about you.

Another way to become memorable or worthy of a story is to solve problems that are outside your area of expertise. I once worked with a housekeeper who helped Marriott win a million-dollar account because she solved such a problem.

The story, which is still being told today, goes like this: The housekeeper was cleaning the room of a program attendee for a major technology corporation when she noticed that the guest had left a suit jacket on the desk chair with a matching button on top of the desk. The housekeeper took it upon herself to sew the button back on the jacket after she finished cleaning the room.

Not being well-versed in English, the housekeeper asked me to write a note on her behalf to the guest, explaining what she had done. Her intention was to apologize in advance if the guest thought this was in any way an invasion of her privacy. I think the housekeeper was also looking to promote herself, as I was her boss at the time.

The guest was so thrilled with the housekeeper that she wrote a letter to Mr. Marriott, praising the initiative she had taken. The guest also shared the story with the person who was in charge of all of lodging and travel for the technology company. It turns out that the host hotel was full and this group of attendees had been placed at the Marriott almost by chance. That was the last time that happened. The head of lodging and travel immediately called Marriott's national sales team and arranged for every seminar in the Westchester County, New York, area to be held at the Marriott.

Creating a positive emotional experience, self-promotion, leaving something behind, and solving problems outside your area of expertise are all great ways to generate buzz in support of your own personal brand. They resonate with the people in the local communities you are trying to reach, and they reinforce the power of your personal brand. In short, it's your job to generate these types of stories every single day.

THE LUCKY SEVEN

Once you've given repeaters fodder for their stories about you, it's time to look to the stories that have the depth to carry beyond one community and appeal to repeaters in multiple communities, to boosters, and to the media.

There are seven different types of stories that capture the attention of the media, and that will surely capture the attention of repeaters and boosters as long as they are true, make an emotional connection, and are tales that can relate to their own lives. These "Lucky Seven" are:

Sex, Lies, and the Outrageous

Howard Stern is the master of this category. He gets press and plenty of buzz just because people want to hear what he will say next. Although some are offended by stories of sex or lies or the outrageous—everyone listens to them or watches them on television. The things you shouldn't talk about have a way of captivating everyone when you do talk about them.

The Who-Dun-It

Everyone loves a good mystery, especially when real life consequences are associated with its resolution. Stories like Natalee Holloway's disappearance in Aruba or the Washington, D.C.–area sniper keep audiences captivated because there are consequences associated with solving—or not solving—the mystery.

The Hype

The media loves stories that are built up with anticipation. Each year, the Super Bowl is one of the most hyped events in the world. Super Bowl Sunday includes a pre-game show that lasts over seven hours. There are news stories about the news stories that cover this event.

An additional benefit of having a story that has enormous hype associated with it is that there are always a few stories afterward about whether or not the story lived up to its advanced billing.

The Cinderella Story

The opposite of the hype story is the underdog or Cinderella story. This is a story that depicts an impossible challenge for an individual, a group, or a team. Everyone loves to root for these folks to beat the odds. Often the subject of this story will be positioned as someone who has been underestimated or counted out. Because most people feel underestimated and undervalued, this story has great public appeal.

The 1980 United States Olympic hockey team is a classic Cinderella Story. No one ever expected them to beat the Soviet Union and then go on to win a gold medal.

The Hilarious

If you can make people laugh, you can win their hearts. People love stories that make them laugh. This is particularly powerful when people poke fun at themselves. A self-deprecating story makes even the biggest star seem down-to-earth.

Larry David, the creator of *Seinfeld* and *Curb Your Enthusiasm*, is the master of this technique. He is incredibly wealthy, yet he regularly makes fun of himself. Audiences show their appreciation by watching his shows—over and over and over again.

The Hero

The story of the hero or the comeback is another favorite. When regular people rise up and do something unexpected, it almost always makes news.

The story of Bethany Hamilton, the young surfer from Hawaii who lost her arm to a shark attack, had people the world over touting her as a role model and an inspiration for persevering and continuing her surfing career.

The Secrets

Everyone loves secrets. People all over the country—and around the world—were riveted to their televisions, newspapers, and computers when U.S. President Bill Clinton was embroiled in a secret relationship with Monica Lewinsky. As the secret unraveled, people clamored to get as much information as possible.

How can you take advantage of these "lucky seven" story types? If you find yourself in a situation that can benefit your business—or if your competitor gets caught up in a negative story—you can spread the news at the grassroots level. You can be sure repeaters will pick it up, and it may even make it to boosters.

Chapter Nine

BECOME A MASTER PERSUADER

It doesn't matter whether you are meeting with someone face-to-face, over the telephone, or via videoconference—you need to be able to convince him that you can provide him with something of value. Intrepreneurs, Entrepreneurs, and everyone who aspires to become either must be able to communicate and sell his ideas to others. The first step in this process is to have a quality product. In this case, the product is you and the value you can provide.

One of the fundamental principles of Career Intensity is to demonstrate your value to your customers. There is no better opportunity for value demonstration than when you have a big idea and you need to share it with your customers or your boss. Just expressing this idea in a clear, coherent fashion will not be enough to make it a reality. You must sell it to them. You must persuade your constituents that you are credible and that your idea is the best thing they have ever heard.

The need to sell is universal. Everyone in the workforce—whether he is working in a company or as an entrepreneur—needs to be able to influence the behavior of others in a favorable way. In short, everyone sells. So, becoming a master persuader can be helpful in a myriad of situations:

Making a Case for Financing—Entrepreneurs need to secure financing to make their business dreams a reality. In order to obtain the capital necessary to start or expand a business, you must have a solid business plan and you must be able to convince others that your plan will succeed.

Intrepreneurs need to secure financing for internal initiatives. Most of these negotiations occur during budget planning. Many good ideas die a slow and painful death because a manager is unable to persuade her boss of the merits of funding and implementing them.

Motivating Employees—There is no such thing as blind faith when it comes to managing employees. The command-and-control style of management just doesn't cut it anymore. Even the U.S. Armed Forces is teaching soldiers the "Why" behind the orders. Selling vs. telling is the way to combine leadership with development. This is true for those in corporate roles as well as for Entrepreneurs.

Winning over the majority of the group—especially in cross-functional work teams—is an approach that results in improved productivity and increased dedication and loyalty. Employees who buy into management's approach to the task at hand will put greater effort into their work. This effort is transparent to customers and often translates into higher sales and profitability.

Creating Alliances—Persuasion is critical in creating alliances among peers or potential business partners. Having friends or allies is valuable in companies large and small. In order to create alliances, you need to be able to persuade others that you are the type of person who will provide them with value.

Building Teams—Every business can benefit from improved teamwork. Persuasion is a critical component in helping create teams and in keeping teams working together. A team has to adopt a unified mindset to achieve a goal. Individuals need to be convinced that the team's goal is beneficial to them as well. This requires persuasion.

Getting a New Job—If you are in the large segment of the population that is unhappy at work, then you will, undoubtedly, be looking for a new job at some point in the future. A job interview is nothing more than a sales meeting. It is an opportunity to sell yourself. You must persuade your target (the hiring manager) that you are the best thing to ever happen to his company.

To sell yourself, your products, or your ideas, you need to become a master persuader. This means that you must understand how people think, act, and make decisions. You need to learn how to influence people so that you can win them over to your way of thinking, yet effective persuasion is both a skill and a responsibility. Before you can learn to persuade others, you need to understand the Rules of the Road for master persuaders.

RULES OF THE ROAD

Your career is fragile. Your personal brand can take a serious hit if your reputation is damaged in any way. Personal contact with others—particularly when you are trying to convince them to take action—is a moment of truth for your personal brand. You need to be extra careful when managing these interactions. The five rules to guide you are:

Rule 1: Believe in yourself and have faith in the quality of your product. The foundation for reinforcing your brand during the sales process is a belief in the quality of your product. If you're an Entrepreneur and you don't believe in what you're selling, then you are working in a fantasyland. If you're an Intrepreneur in the workplace, you must believe in the task at hand—or at least in its potential—in order to feel good about selling it to someone else.

Back when I was a catering service manager in a hotel, I'd often be asked for advice on selecting a wedding planner. Having worked with several outstanding event planners, I'd always encourage clients to interview prospective event planners by asking them to describe their daughter's wedding. I would tell the couple to watch the enthusiasm and passion with which the wedding planner described the event. The more passion and the more detail she provided, the better the wedding planner. Someone with passion for their product, service, or themselves is authentic and the kind of person with whom you want to work. Likewise, you should feel passionate about yourself and your business when you are trying to persuade someone else to work with you. If you don't believe in yourself, you can't, in good conscience, ask others to believe in you.

Rule 2: All of your dealings must be moral, ethical, and legal. Each interaction you have in persuading others must meet all three conditions. You have to be able to look yourself in the mirror after every interaction. You should be proud to tell others about a deal you made with a prospective client, coworker, or employer. You should never feel embarrassed by your actions while trying to convince people to work with you.

A good test for moral, legal, and ethical persuasion techniques is to ask yourself how you would feel if the entire sales process were exposed, word-for-word, on the front page of the *New York Times*. If the thought sends chills down your spine, chances are that your technique violates this rule.

Rule 3: Your efforts in persuasion must follow The Golden Rule. Do unto others as you would have them do unto you. No one likes to feel as though they were played for a fool. You should approach any interaction where persuasion comes into play as though you'll be treated the same way in the future. Call it business karma. What goes around comes around.

There is a difference between persuasion and manipulation, as well as between persuasion and coercion. Persuasion means influencing the opinion of another person. Manipulation implies that a devious act is involved in the persuasion process. Coercion implies that force or intimidation is involved while influencing the other party to make a decision.

There is no place for manipulation or coercion in the process of selling yourself. Both will lead to long-term resentment. There is no way a productive relationship can be built on a shaky foundation. You'll undoubtedly have the opportunity to use information to your advantage to influence a person's opinion. Resist using coercive or manipulative tactics to achieve your goals. You will not only be a better person for it, but you will also strike fear in the hearts of those who rely on this type of behavior to close deals.

There will always be opportunities to take advantage of someone else. In the end, you need to be able to live with the consequences of your own actions. You never know when you will work with—or for—someone else.

We recently investigated a technology solution for our company. We received a number of bids that made the solution appear complicated and expensive. In comparison, the last bid we evaluated was extremely low. We invited that company to formally pitch to us. The company turned out to be a sole proprietor named John who worked from home. He explained that his bid was for introducing us to a company that would provide us with everything we would need for one-tenth the price of our next lowest bid. He stated that his honesty would probably cost him thousands, but he could not, in good conscience, take our money for just introducing us to someone else. We gave him a small finder's fee for the time he put into researching the issue.

John saved us thousands of dollars. The next time we have an issue with our computers, whom do you think we will call?

Rule 4: The other person must always leave the interaction with her dignity intact. There will come a time in your career where people will be told to work with you because they have to; or you will win a big negotiation; or you will have the upper hand and have to work with the person with whom you competed. In these situations, you need to allow the other person to maintain her dignity.

This opportunity often presents itself when another person first realizes that you're selling the only solution to her problem. Although you have the opportunity to make them look foolish, don't do it. Instead, allow them to save face.

As an executive with Marriott, I once had a colleague with whom I shared an acrimonious relationship. He completely dressed me down in front of a room full of other executives when he launched an attack on a strategy that I had devised. His passion for his case overwhelmed the facts. The foundation of his argument was based upon some numbers that were outdated by about six months. The new numbers (which were released just days prior to the meeting—while my colleague was on vacation) rendered his argument useless and my strategy totally on point.

After my colleague finished his impassioned speech, I asked for a brief break in the meeting. As people milled about, getting coffee and stretching their legs, I privately informed my colleague of the new figures. He spent several minutes arguing that the new figures could not have been released yet and then he left the room—presumably to check on the information I gave him.

He returned to the room at the end of the break and immediately admitted his mistake to the entire group.

Later that evening, I was waiting for an elevator and this colleague caught up to me. He thanked me for addressing the issue with him directly, and he told me that my behavior was "one of the classiest things I've ever seen." That man and I were never at odds again. We did not always agree, but he always gave me the benefit of the doubt when I tried to win him over to my side of an argument.

Think of the other way that situation could have unfolded. I could have dropped the bombshell on him in the meeting, in front of everyone. I could have made him look foolish and stripped him of his dignity. In the future, if I need something from him, how do you think he will react?

Rule 5: The best ideas are their ideas. It's astonishing how much work you can get done if you allow others to take the credit. It's even more powerful when the other party believes that the magic idea was theirs in the first place.

The consulting business is all about solving problems and allowing others to take credit for your solutions. We call this "external orientation." You have to be willing to give your ideas to others in order to make certain that you acquire and retain business. You need to educate your clients on the solutions you have devised for them so that they can speak knowledgeably to their boss and their customers about them.

In the end, you will know that you have made an impression on someone when they begin to internalize your solutions. Sometimes they do this consciously and sometimes you have made such a strong case that they have adopted your point of view without even realizing it. Either way, your position gets adopted and you win. That's not a bad deal.

When you work for someone, either a boss or a client, your job is to make that person look good. Sometimes it's tough. Your reward will be a higher perception of value in the eyes of that person.

The more you make your boss look good, the more he will be dependent upon you. If he is dependent upon you, he will want to keep you happy. In the case of a client, your reward will be more business or more difficult problems to solve.

DIRECT VS. INDIRECT INFORMATION PROCESSING

Have you ever tried to win someone over to your way of thinking with a well-reasoned argument that just did not work? You made what you thought was the perfect case. You lined up all of your information. You presented it as clearly as possible. Your argument was supported by a good deal of data. You informed the audience of the benefits they would receive if they followed your guidance. And then nothing happened. The audience did not buy the information (or the product) you were selling. Where did you go wrong? Chances are, you weren't communicating information to your audience in a way they wanted to receive it.

Persuasive messages are processed in two different ways. Sometimes people process our persuasive message directly. The receiver listens to what we are saying. He thinks about the facts and considers the points of our argument. He carefully weighs all of the evidence and comes to a decision. The second way is indirect and more passive. In what is known as the peripheral route, the message is less of a focus. The receiver relies on cues that he is receiving to help him judge whether the message is valid and if he should believe the premises of the argument. The number of arguments or examples presented or the appearance of the speaker makes a big difference for those who process persuasive messages through this indirect or peripheral route.

Generally, you employ both types of information processing on a daily basis. Two primary factors determine what information travels down which route in your brain. The first is motivation. If you are interested in the topic being presented, you are more likely to process the information directly. You spend more time considering each of the factors involved in evaluating the argument, and you may ask questions to gain a better understanding of the concepts involved.

If you are not interested in the information that is being presented—if your motivation is low—you are more likely to use the peripheral route to process the information. You won't spend a lot of time thinking through arguments; instead, subtle cues play a role in your decision. Instead of agonizing over a decision, you make a quick judgment and move on to the next activity.

Take the example of someone who has worked all of his life for an annual salary of $25,000. If he suddenly wins $10 million in the lottery, he is far more motivated to understand tax shelters and the benefits of investing in tax-free municipal bonds than he was previously. Likewise, someone who is about to jump out of a plane is far more motivated to understand the aerodynamics involved in the operation of a parachute than someone who never has any intention of skydiving.

The second factor that determines which route information takes when being processed is cognitive ability or intelligence. If you can't gain a full understanding of the information that is presented, you'll have a difficult time actively processing it. Although intelligence is a significant factor in your ability to comprehend information being presented, experience in a specific area can also determine your motivation or level of involvement in receiving the message. I know several college professors who are highly intelligent but who absolutely cannot fix their cars. The knowledge required to fix an automobile largely comes from experience. Even though my professor friends would have the ability to understand the concepts involved in fixing their vehicles, it's unlikely that they would be motivated to do so because they lack the experience that would allow them to jump right into the project. It is likely that they would be more susceptible to the peripheral method of information processing when choosing a mechanic to repair their automobiles.

Although there's not a definitive theory as to why we have developed two methods of processing information, the popular assumption is that we are bombarded with hundreds of thousands of pieces of information on a daily basis. Because the stimuli are too numerous to consciously process, our minds have developed cues that help us make calculated guesses based upon past experience.

These cues make up the peripheral route of decision making many people take when someone is trying to persuade them.

One example of mental cues in action is how people perceive you based upon your appearance. Whenever I travel on business, I always make it a point to wear business attire. It is interesting to notice that the reaction of the people with whom I interact is based upon how I am dressed. I find that I am more likely to get upgraded (or to get onto a flight if flying standby) if I am wearing a business suit than if I am wearing jeans and a T-shirt. I also receive more attentive service while on the airplane and when I arrive at the hotel. Appearance—in this case wearing a suit—is a cue to others that I am a businessperson or someone of value to their business.

Another example of an appearance cue in action is the power of a uniform. Doctors and police officers wear uniforms to help convey a sense of expertise and authority to the public. Uniforms can do much more than that. When I was 21 years old, I was a hotel bellman. I wore a very ugly, double-breasted uniform that was made of itchy wool. No one could mistake me for anything but a bellman. Yet, that uniform had a certain magical power. Anytime someone asked me for something or needed my help, they gave me money. If someone needed directions, I got a buck. If someone needed a car door opened, I got another buck. If I carried their bags, I got a couple of bucks. If I helped with a dinner reservation, I got five bucks.

During the year I worked in that job, I never asked anyone for a tip. It was implied. People saw the uniform and they instantly understood that I was working for tips. A natural cue was triggered in their minds.

I would often change clothes after work and walk up the street to a local diner to get something to eat. There were many times when people asked me for directions as I walked out of the hotel's employee entrance. Not one of those times did I receive a tip. The only difference was that I was wearing street clothes and not the uniform. The cues differ as one's appearance changes. Had I tried to close a big real estate deal in that bellman uniform, I might have had a difficult time.

How Does Your Target Process Information?

In everyday situations, people use both the direct and indirect methods of processing information. Although they switch back and forth regularly, individuals will generally favor one method over the other. In order to persuade your target that your idea or product is valuable, you must be able to assess the method of information processing that he is using. By taking the following steps, you can adjust your communication strategy to align with his method of processing information:

Understand her frame of mind. People who are adept at reading their audience are more likely to be effective persuaders. To assess your target's frame of mind, first observe her behavior. Generally speaking, if your listener is attentive, alert, and thoughtful, you can begin to assume she is processing information via the direct route. If she starts to appear distracted or bored, you can assume that she is processing information via the indirect route.

Ask your target some questions, and when she answers, judge the quality of her responses. If they sound sensible and reasonable, she's probably processing information using the direct route. If she asks you to repeat the question or gives answers that don't fit in with the overall conversation, she's relying on peripheral cues.

When people are in the direct mode of information processing, they look and act differently than when they are in the indirect mode. You can practice getting a feel for each by staging discussions with people about topics outside of their chosen fields or professions. For example, if you have a conversation with an artist who does not like sports and ask questions like, "Did you know that Ron Guidry struck out 18 batters in a game on June 17, 1978? Did you know that he had a career record of 170 wins and 91 losses? Did you know that his career-earned run average was 3.29?" her reactions will be telling. Most likely, she'll appear disconnected and judge what you are saying based upon your enthusiasm rather than on the value of the information. Her eyes may seem unfocused or dart around, her body language may be languid, or she may tap her foot impatiently. She's processing information indirectly. If you change the subject to the new exhibit at the Museum of Modern Art, though, she'll likely snap to attention, become actively engaged in the conversation, and bring her expertise and passion to the discussion. She's switched to the direct information-processing mode.

Match your technique to his mental state. Just as you don't need sunglasses at night, you don't need to make a logical argument to someone who processes most of his information using the indirect mental route. Although it's irritating to develop thoughtful arguments or cues and then see them fail because you used them at the wrong time, you must coordinate your method of persuasion to match his mental state.

When in doubt, take the indirect route. In most situations, your listener will lapse into the indirect mode of information processing. It is just easier for her to let information wash over her and allow her automated systems to steer her. Despite this tendency, most people make persuasive arguments as if their listener were always in the direct mode, ready to receive intense and logical arguments. All too often, they design their pitches or presentations assuming that their receivers are ready to handle the features, benefits, and statistics they have to offer.

Always think of the indirect route as your listener's default mode. If you are uncertain which mode your listener is using to receive information, it is always best to incorporate indirect triggers into your presentation. Strategies to appeal to indirect information processing will never be harmful in a presentation to a receiver who is in direct mode. You will simply need to include a rational argument in your presentation to that person. To take the reverse approach—making a rational argument to an indirect thinker—is to waste time and energy and will possibly confuse the situation. When in doubt, take the indirect route.

Make your case from the receiver's point of view. Persuasion is no different than other areas where you have to look at a situation from the viewpoint of your customer. Because the process of effective persuasion is based upon the needs of your customer, you must develop arguments from his point of view.

Unfortunately, we tend to rely on the belief that the other person will respond to our arguments the way we would. This is no different than the ten-year-old boy who found a great gift for his mom's birthday—a hockey stick. We must construct arguments that are compelling and powerful to our listeners, rather than develop them to suit our own tastes.

The best way to develop good arguments is to carefully observe your listener. Really listen to him. Ask him about his likes and dislikes. Pay attention to the clothes he wears and the language he uses. Construct your arguments to match his ability and willingness to receive information. This will help you make the connection necessary to win him over to your point of view.

CREDIBILITY EQUALS SUCCESS

In effective persuasion, the person who is presenting the information is just as important as whether the case appeals to the listener's direct or indirect approach to information processing. It all comes down to credibility—how believable the person communicating the message is in the eyes of the audience.

When thinking about credibility, keep four factors in mind. First, know that credibility is in the eyes of the receiver. The perception of the message's intended receiver is all that matters. If that person finds the sender believable, the sender has credibility.

Second, credibility is multidimensional. Honesty, integrity, experience, skill, knowledge, and the duration of the relationship with the receiver all contribute to the perception of credibility that one person has for another. Changes in any or all of these dimensions can add or detract from the perception of an individual's credibility.

Third, credibility is situational. Just as a car mechanic wouldn't have credibility in repairing a broken leg, a doctor wouldn't have credibility in evaluating problems with a brake rotor on a Honda. In his own setting, the mechanic and the doctor each has credibility. Once they are removed from that context, their credibility can dramatically decrease.

Finally, credibility can change over time. A dramatic example of how credibility can change is the case of Rafael Palmeiro. On March 17, 2005, Rafael Palmeiro of the Baltimore Orioles told a congressional committee that he never used performance-enhancing steroids. On July 15 of that year, Palmeiro reached a baseball milestone. He got the 3,000th hit of his then-distinguished career; something accomplished by only 25 other players in the history of the game. On August 1, 2005, the 40-year-old Palmeiro was suspended from the team when a drug test found traces of steroids in his system. During this short period of time, Palmeiro's credibility as one of the all-time great hitters in baseball had been crushed. In July, Palmeiro was considered one of the best, and two weeks later, he was regarded as a cheater.

Deciding whether to present information directly or indirectly is a moot point if you don't have credibility. The direct processor of information will receive and immediately process information presented by an individual with high credibility. Rightfully so, she will spend less time questioning the validity of that information and more time thinking about the content of the message.

The indirect information processor will accept the information as true when it is presented by someone with high credibility. She will also be more likely to agree to a recommendation made by someone with high credibility without questioning the details of the suggestion.

Primary Dimensions of Credibility

Research has shown that there are three primary dimensions of credibility: expertise, trustworthiness, and goodwill.

Expertise. This tells the world that you know your stuff. Expertise is usually gained through the acquisition of skills and knowledge, or through experience. Sometimes, a title alone is enough to provide the perception of expertise. Designations such as M.D., Ph.D., or CPA often allow individuals to claim significant levels of expertise in specific subjects or professions.

In the world of persuasion, perception can often become reality. In the case of titles, an unscrupulous person could add a title or designation to her name with the hope of influencing others' perceptions of her credibility. In most cases, this person would suffer irrevocable damage to her credibility if this fraud were discovered. Since you are interested in winning the hearts and minds of your clients for the long term, the implications of faking it are too severe to ever warrant such an attempt.

Experience in a specific field will often allow you to claim expertise in that area. The casino industry often employs former cheats—people who have experience in defrauding casinos—to help test systems designed to prevent cheating and catch cheaters. These people derive their expertise from their years of experience in this dubious line of work.

Trustworthiness. A communicator must convey the perception of honesty and integrity to his audience in order for them to believe the message he is trying to convey.

One of the most reliable tools a communicator can use in attempting to convey trustworthiness to his audience is time. If a communicator's actions match his words over a period of time, the perception of his trustworthiness will grow. Sustained, consistent performance over time will help enhance his reputation as a trustworthy person.

Another way a communicator can help increase his listeners' feelings of trustworthiness is through positive performance during a major event or situation. A cab driver that finds a bag containing $60,000 and then turns that bag over to authorities is going to be perceived as an honest person. The performance of the individual in this extreme situation helps develop his reputation as a person who is worthy of trust.

Goodwill. In order to be perceived as a nice person or a good person, a communicator must communicate that she cares about her audience. This caring can be demonstrated by taking a genuine interest in the receiver of the message. Showing concern for another person's needs, thoughts, or ideas is also important in demonstrating goodwill. Displaying empathy toward someone or an individual's situation also leads to an increased perception of goodwill.

Sometimes it is sufficient to say that you feel the pain of your audience. The perception of goodwill can also be extended to individuals who have been through similar experiences. At funerals, a person who has recently lost a loved one can be a pillar of strength to the grieving family. There is a perceived bond created by the ability of that individual to feel the pain of the grieving family.

A politician often plays up the feelings he had when growing up under difficult circumstances. This is an attempt to create goodwill among his constituents. In this case, the politician is demonstrating the shared feelings that he experienced with potential voters. Again, this is a time for exercising caution. If you are disingenuous in any way in demonstrating care and concern for others, you will lose them for good. Demonstrating goodwill and empathy is not something you can fake over the long term.

Secondary Dimensions of Credibility

Other dimensions of credibility are situation-specific. Focusing on these areas will sometimes lead to success in enhancing your credibility, and sometimes it will not. If you are attempting to create a long-term relationship, it is helpful to understand the complete credibility picture. It can never hurt to keep the secondary dimensions of credibility in mind as you approach your next potential relationship.

High dynamic energy is a quality that many superachievers share. People are naturally drawn to others who are full of life and energy. Being animated and enthusiastic is helpful in winning them over.

High energy can influence the perception of credibility in two different ways. One is the electric sense of activity that surrounds the person who has such energy. The second is that the dynamic person's energy rubs off on others and inspires them to go out and get things done. You must, however, be careful to match your level of energy to the situation. For example, it would be inappropriate to appear overwhelmingly excited after your team loses a big account.

Another secondary source of credibility is composure or grace under pressure. People are not only comforted by a controlled presence in stressful situations, but they are also drawn to it. Your work in strategic thinking and contingency planning will help you maintain your cool in difficult situations. This will serve you well in stressful situations, and others will look to you for help.

For many top performers, sociability is an additional source of credibility. I recently attended an event at Columbia University and watched as several students went out of their way to greet one student in particular. Realizing that I had an opportunity to meet several new people at once just by meeting her, I approached this student and introduced myself. She was pleasant and made me feel at ease. After we chatted for a few minutes, she introduced me to 12 other people. Her introduction gave me credibility within their group because she endorsed me.

Enhancing Your Credibility

Now that you understand credibility and how it can benefit you, it's time to find ways to enhance or improve your credibility. Again, keep in mind that it's the perception of the receiver that is important. Just because a strategy works on you doesn't mean that it will work on someone else.

In making your case to an audience, you must first establish your own credibility before making your argument. You will have an opportunity to win them over—either through the direct or indirect route of persuasion—later on. The first objective is to make them see you as someone they believe. Here are some steps you can take to make that happen:

Be prepared. Make certain that your case is well thought through and that you have identified the key points before making your presentation. Emphasize your key points quickly and succinctly. Do not overly complicate the issues. An organized, brief message is critical. Then, cite evidence for your position. Anytime you can quote specific information that supports your argument, you will enhance your credibility. Make sure to cite your own experience in the subject matter. Expertise is a primary dimension of credibility, so speak from personal experience—with detail—whenever possible.

Demonstrate honesty and sincerity. If you make a mistake, admit it. If you don't know the answer, say so. If someone asks why you are there, tell him. If I am on a sales call and someone asks me why I am there, I will say something like, "To win your business." If the conversation has been lighthearted, I might say, "To try to make us both some money." This is honest and sincere, and it has changed the dynamics of many discussions.

Be a person of goodwill. Don't be arrogant or aloof. Let people know that you understand their situation. Share a personal tidbit about yourself that shows some commonality with your audience. I work with a gentleman who has beautiful twins. Whenever we go into an office where a client has pictures of children around, my coworker asks about the children. "How old are they? Is this a recent picture? They look just like you." The client then asks if he has children, and he briefly talks about his twin girls. If he is able to show their school pictures, I immediately know that we will have an easy time discussing business with this client. The common ground has already been established, and we are in an environment of goodwill.

Use language that fits the audience. Don't use slang or jargon. Never, ever use off-color language. Match the rate of speed and tone of your voice to that of your client. Choppy sentences and "Ums" and "Uh-huhs" are bad.

Don't qualify your statements. Don't say things like, "I think this is a great color, don't you?" State your position with authority and with your full support, as in "This is a great color."

Have someone with high credibility introduce you. It is always powerful to have someone who the client respects make an introduction for you. This can often serve as an implied endorsement.

TAKING THE DIRECT ROUTE

Several different approaches work with individuals who process information in a logical and thoughtful way. All of these approaches involve knowing your facts. You can't enter into an environment that calls for persuasion without a thorough understanding of the facts involved in the situation.

As you prepare your case, you need to keep in mind that the fewer points you have to make, the more powerful the argument for each point will appear to the receiver. The power of each argument is diffused if there are multiple arguments. You never want to make more than three points in any persuasive session. Three is the optimal number because people can always remember a list with three items on it. Often, something gets lost on the way from three to five or more.

As you pare down your ideas to get to your three critical points, you need to ask yourself some difficult questions. Consider, for example:

- What do you want your target—your audience—to do?
- What is the best possible outcome for you?
- How does this outcome fit in with your target's goals?
- How does your solution solve your target's problem?
- What values do you and the target share?
- How can you link the benefits of your solution to all aspects of your target's work?
- Can you answer the "So what?" question?
- Can you answer the questions, "Why?" or "Why not?"

You must be prepared with answers to these questions when you plan your direct appeal to your target. This appeal must have a logical and rational flow, but it must also link the rational benefits to the emotions and values that are important to your target.

I take a four-point approach when making a case using a direct route: position, problem, possibilities, and proposal.

Position. Begin by framing the background. Be as specific as possible. Summarize the facts of the case briefly, with no editorializing. Be sure to include only items that can be stipulated—that all parties agree are facts.

Problem. Describe why the current state will not be effective in the future. Highlight the ways in which this is causing (or is going to cause) pain to your audience. This is critical. You must link the facts to pain for the person on the receiving end of your message. Remember—you need to make it about them.

Possibilities. Next, outline the possible solutions to the problem. You need to help them see how you can help take the pain away. Your list of possibilities should never number more than three. The first item on the list should be the solution that is least pleasing to you. When you present it, you need to appear objective, fair, and balanced. The final possibility you present should be the argument you favor the most. You should have a number of facts to support your position.

Proposal. This is the step where you specifically outline how you would implement your proposed solution. Once you reach this point in the argument, you need to listen to the other party very carefully. There may be some elements of your solution that he doesn't care for, but there could be other parts he finds acceptable. This is when you need to modify your position to make it more acceptable to your target.

The goal is for you to reach the middle ground between your ideal situation and the situation that would be ideal for the other side. The closer you are to a solution that addresses the primary needs of both parties, and that concedes minor points, the better off you will be.

In a sales scenario, you will be provided with compensation (money) and the audience (the client) will be provided with a service. The ideal situation is that, the more compensation you receive, the more service the client receives. You may hear people say that the objective is to give less service for more money. I disagree. The best deals are those that are equitable. That is why listening is important.

TAKING THE INDIRECT ROUTE

When it comes to the indirect route of persuasion, there are a number of common misconceptions. The primary one is that the indirect route is deceptive or coercive. This does not need to be the case. At one time or another, everyone has used the peripheral process (the indirect route) of decision making. In selling your ideas or persuading people, you are only being deceptive if you are convincing them to do something that is not in their best interest.

The indirect route is helpful when you are not certain what level of engagement you have with your audience. If your target isn't interested in the details of a direct approach, or they don't need the detail involved in a direct approach, you should use indirect tactics. In addition, it will never hurt your case to pair direct arguments with indirect tactics.

Remember that indirect persuasion is designed to trigger a specific reaction in the subconscious mind of your target. Ultimately, people exercise their own free will in making decisions. Your persuasive tactics will make it easier for them to make a decision and feel good about doing it.

TACTICS USED BY MASTER PERSUADERS

People with Career Intensity are masters of persuasion. They almost always understand their target audiences, understand the viewpoints of the people they are trying to persuade, and understand how to present an idea, product, or service so that both they and their target's needs are met.

Intrepreneurs and Entrepreneurs use powerful techniques of persuasion. In order to form agreements and alliances, you would do well to add the following tools to your persuasion arsenal:

Give to Get

Generally, we are unaware of the power of implied obligation. Every time I go to a wedding, I am reminded of this powerful tactic. Whenever I write out the card that goes along with a gift to a new bride and groom, I can't help but think about the gift that they gave me at my wedding. If they did not attend my wedding, I think about the elaborate affair they're planning for their wedding celebration. I think about what they are spending to make sure their guests will enjoy the day. Subconsciously, I feel an obligation to repay these folks for the gifts they have given me or are about to give me.

This is a powerful psychological phenomenon that has been around since the days when cavemen organized themselves into villages. If there was someone in the village who was in need, the other members of the tribe pitched in to help him. At the heart of this concept was an implied understanding that the tribe member who benefited would pitch in to help others when the circumstances warranted.

This concept still exists today. When someone gives you something, you feel an obligation to repay her with a favor in return. Sometimes this obligation can weigh heavily on your mind like a strange form of guilt. The need to return the favor can be so powerful that it can magnify itself over time. This will often cause you, the recipient of the original favor, to go well beyond what would be considered appropriate in paying back the provider.

Likewise, when you give something to someone or when you share resources, you subconsciously feel as though you have earned a credit. You do not feel as though you are actually giving something away.

This phenomenon is also at work in a corporate setting. I recently spoke with a pharmaceutical sales representative named Michael about his sales process. I asked him how he could convince doctors to write prescriptions for his company's products instead of his competitors' products. This industry is fiercely competitive and the product he sold was comparable to all of the other products on the market. Michael told me that his sales style was all about relationships. He told me a story that demonstrates implied obligation in action.

Michael was trying to win over a doctor who, for years, had been writing prescriptions for a competitor's product. He went to see this doctor twice a month for the first six months he was on the job. One day, during a casual conversation, the doctor brought up the fact that he was leaving on vacation early the next Sunday morning. Knowing that it would be difficult to get a family member to get up at 4:00 a.m. on a Sunday to drive the doctor to the airport, Michael offered to pick the doctor up and take him in his own car. The doctor was thrilled. Subconsciously, the doctor had obligated himself to Michael for that ride. That doctor is now Michael's number one customer.

You can use this principle to your advantage almost every day. Doing so is as easy as knowing what to say when you have just done a favor for someone. After the favor is complete and the person says, "Thank you," you have an opportunity. Your opportunity is to keep that social contract intact and say something to the effect of, "I'm glad to do it because I know that you'd do the same thing for me." In this way, you acknowledge the system and you maintain the relationship that will allow them to return the favor.

Keeping Up with the Crowd

We all find it easier to do what other people are doing because we value the validation we receive for our social behavior.

Back in December 1998, I was riding the subway during the holiday season. Just as the doors of the train opened at a busy station, a woman screamed that someone had stolen her purse. The entire subway car full of people watched as a man rapidly pushed and shoved his way through the crowd with the woman's purse in hand. Not one person did anything. It was as though the group were frozen.

What made everyone in the group remain fixed in their places? The most likely answer is uncertainty. When we are uncertain as to what behavior is appropriate in a given situation, we will likely follow the crowd. In this case, the crowd did nothing. We all took our cues from one another. As long as nobody helped, nobody would help.

I came across another instance of this behavior while at a New York Jets football game some years ago. The game had ended and an entire parking lot full of cars had been blocked in by an inconsiderate fan who had parked directly in front of the exit. The only way to exit this portion of the parking lot was to drive over a concrete island that was about 18 inches high. Several cars begin to hop the curb and drive over the island. The situation became somewhat more complicated when the cars reached the other side. There was a large puddle that had been created as the result of a rainstorm. This puddle was up against the curb of the concrete island. The drivers of the cars could not tell how steep the drop-off between the island and the ground was because they did not know the depth of the puddle.

The first two vehicles to go over the island were trucks, and they made it with absolutely no problem. The next vehicle to attempt this feat was a small car with a narrow wheelbase. Bam— the car's bottom struck the curb and its muffler ripped off. The noise this made drew some onlookers. The frustrated and embarrassed driver of the small car drove off after picking up his muffler. The next few vehicles made it over the curb with little difficulty. Finally, a vehicle with several young women approached the end of the island with some hesitancy. The group that had gathered around began chanting, "Go, go, go!" so the young lady in the driver's seat gave the vehicle some gas and—Bam— her car also struck bottom but managed to make it over the curb.

Several dozen cars drove over that concrete island and three of them lost various parts of their undercarriage. What made people think that they could safely make it across the island and out of the parking lot? Again, it is the principle of social proof— following the crowd—but in this case, the social proof was driven by the similarity of the members of the group. They were all in vehicles. They all had the feeling that what one person can do, another can do. It was this similarity that led these folks to follow the crowd.

How can you use this principle of social proof to your benefit? In truth, you already do it all the time. Anytime you say something like, "Everybody is going" or "All my friends have one," you are using this principal to help you make your case. It is even used by people who market books. The next time you are in a bookstore, look at some of the books that are selling well. You will notice that some of them have a banner or a sticker that says, "Best Seller" or "Over 1 Million Copies Sold." If everyone is buying these books, they must be good.

Commitment and Follow-Through

When someone says one thing and then does another, we think of that person as two-faced or dishonest. The best thing that is often said about them is that they are indecisive or confused. Society places a high value on consistency. A person who commits to doing something and then follows through is considered to be honorable, or a person of her word. Consistency is also associated with logic and rational behavior. A person who is consistent is considered to be honest and stable.

A few years ago, I met a therapist at a seminar I was attending for work. This was a marketing event and the woman was there to learn how to market her practice more effectively. We began to talk during one of the breaks, and I learned that her specialty was in couples counseling. After discussing our respective careers, I asked her how many times people admitted that they knew before they were married that their partner was not right for them.

The therapist's answer shocked me. She said that, in at least 30 percent of the cases where couples break up, one or both partners admit that they knew that the marriage was not going to work out right from the start. She went on to say that at least another 20 percent of people who are married probably either feel this way and won't admit it or they stay with their spouses anyway. That equals half of all married couples. I asked why she thought people who didn't think the marriage would work would get married anyway. Her answer was that the power of making the commitment was so overwhelming that they thought they could make the marriage work.

If the power of commitment and being consistent with the decision you have made is so strong that it forces people to stick with bad, life-altering decisions, what chance do you have in making decisions that are important, yet not life-altering? Think about the person who promises a boss he will stick it out in a terrible job and then makes his life miserable by doing so. How about the young man who says "Yes" to the purchase of a new car that is $5,000 above his price limit and then will not go back on his word to the car dealer? These are situations that all of us face every day as we work hard to live up to our commitments.

How can you, as a master persuader, use this tool to your advantage? One of the best ways to use the power of consistency and commitment is to reinforce successful customer relationships. If a customer is an advocate for you, your product, or your service, she will want to do everything she can to help you succeed. She will want to make certain her words are true. She will provide support to your business in just about any way possible.

Businesses take advantage of the concept of commitment and follow-through with small client-to-client education events. Something magical happens when you introduce your clients to one another. They begin a dialogue around the one thing they have in common—you. Each client has the opportunity to discuss how he is working with you and how you have saved him money, increased his sales, and so forth. Not only do the clients feel like they have joined an exclusive group, but the event also reinforces their relationship with you and your business. They feel a renewed need to continue working with you because, if they do not, they will be inconsistent with the behavior and commitment they demonstrated at the event.

Public displays of commitment are among the most difficult to break. If a client pledges his loyalty to your business publicly, he will do anything in his power to keep that commitment.

The second powerful way that you can use this indirect form of persuasion is through the written word. If you can get a client to write an article in a journal about you, your product, or your service, he will continue the relationship in order to remain consistent with that written commitment. A written document from a client is one of the most powerful and personal forms of commitment.

Listen to Your Friends

It is much easier to say "No" to a stranger than it is to say "No" to a friend. The opposite is also true. People prefer to say "Yes" to those they know and like. Companies like Tupperware, Avon, and Amway are built upon this principle. What happens once you run out of friends? You have to make some new ones to sell more products.

People purchase more products and services from people they like or find attractive. You can create this situation with a stranger by implementing three strategies to get the relationship started off on the right foot.

The first strategy is highlighting similarities between the two of you. These can be personal similarities or business similarities.

You can talk about things that you have in common. You can dress in the same style or taste as your potential customer. If she is a conservative dresser, then you should be reserved in selecting your attire before you meet with her. If she has a fashion-forward style, then you should at least be up on the current trends and be able to display a little flair.

Second, you should be generous but tasteful with you compliments. If you notice that your prospective client takes great pride in her work, be sure and complement something that she has done recently. If you know that her child has won an award, make sure you congratulate her. This may seem like pandering or butt kissing, but it works. You're more likely to work with people who tell you that you are smart, fashionable, trendy, and so on.

The third way to increase the likelihood that a prospect will like you and want to do business with you is to work with them on a collaborative project. If you know that your prospective client is a volunteer for a particular charity, then you should spend some of your free time trying to work with her on a charitable initiative for that group. If you know that your potential customer is on the local school board, then you should take an interest in the town's educational system. Collaborative projects put everyone on the same team—and that is the first step toward a productive relationship.

Listen to the Trusted Advisor

As discussed, people are more likely to be persuaded by someone they perceive to be a trustworthy expert. If you must win someone over and you have never met him before, you can trigger the mental cue for trust by pointing out a weakness in your case. Maybe your product has a flaw. Maybe you lost a customer once.

The way to do this is to present your weakness first and then show how your strong points will overwhelm these weaknesses. You could say something like, "I lost Mr. Jones as a customer because I was so busy that I couldn't guarantee that I would visit him on Wednesday of each week. Some weeks I needed to visit him on Thursdays. I've since hired an assistant who takes care of the paperwork that used to take so much of my time. This has enabled me to keep a consistent schedule. I have kept my fixed visit days with all my clients for the past two years—since hiring the assistant. This is an amazing record of reliability."

By admitting your mistake, you are showing that you are human. Exposing this little flaw allows your customer to see your honesty. That serves as a trigger for trustworthiness, which is a building block of credibility.

Supplies Are Limited

People always want what they can't have. Scarcity creates demand. This is a time-tested principle that lives along the indirect route of persuasion. The New Coke–Old Coke case is a classic example of scarcity enhancing the appeal of a product.

In the early 1980s, Coke was on the verge of losing the cola wars to Pepsi. The company's market share had remained flat for 15 years while Pepsi's steadily increased. Unless the executives at Coca-Cola could come up with the reasons behind the rise in Pepsi's popularity and the flattening of the consumption of their product, Pepsi would be able to claim more people drank their soft drink than Coke. The company was already claiming that people preferred the taste of Pepsi to Coke, and even developed "Pepsi Challenge" commercials to clearly demonstrate this preference. The Coke brain trust had to find out why people were switching to Pepsi.

In the end, it came down to taste. Dozens of well-controlled taste tests showed that folks liked the taste of Pepsi better than the taste of Coke. Adding to the mix of issues was the popularity of Diet Coke. This relatively new beverage was formulated in such a way that it ended up with a taste that was closer Pepsi than to its parent beverage.

What did Coke do? In 1985, they replaced Coca-Cola with "New Coke." This formula was more like the taste of Pepsi, and in the company's market research, people preferred it. The public's reaction shocked everyone at Coca-Cola. People were outraged. They wanted and they demanded to have the "Old Coke" back. The new product replaced the old product on April 23, 1985. Demand for the old product was so strong that the company was forced to announce that it would begin making it again on July 11 of that same year.

Although millions of people were originally outraged at the Coca-Cola's decision, they embraced the company after it announced the decision to return the old beverage. The demand for the original product had convinced many people to give Coke a try. All of this stemmed from the perception of scarcity created when the "Old Coke" was removed from the market. Once people began drinking Coke Classic ("Old Coke" that was reintroduced), they never switched. This mistake—which made Old Coke scarce during the summer of 1985—helped give the brand the boost it needed to regain its dominance in the cola wars.

The way to create the Coke Effect in your business is to explain to people the unique aspect of your product or service. What can't they get anywhere else?

When you explain the scarcity of your product or service to your customer, you have to phrase it in a way that allows her to believe that she will lose something by not purchasing it. She is more likely to react the way you want her to when she perceives there to be a loss associated with inaction. Pain is a stronger motivator than pleasure.

Change Perspective

The final method for triggering a subconscious reaction in your target involves making requests in a specific order so that you can influence the perception of the request you really want.

If you want someone to do you a favor, always ask for a larger favor first. This will frame the request you really want as smaller by comparison. For example, if you really need to borrow $10 from your brother, you are better off asking for $100 first. When you brother refuses, your request for $10 seems small in comparison.

If you want a friend to watch your dog for a couple of days and you are not sure if she will agree, you should first ask if she will watch your dog for a week. When she declines, you can retreat to the two-day request and it will seem like a much less significant favor in comparison. If you have a list of requests, always place the largest one first.

This method is effective, not only because it helps you achieve your ultimate goal, but also because if you get the other party to agree to the larger request, you will look like a hero when you don't need as much help as you originally thought. The key to this entire approach is to make your second request immediately after you are denied the first request. In this way, the two requests are perceived as one event. If you wait too long, the second request will be seen as a new request and you run the risk of being denied once again.

Winning people over to your way of thinking is critical to the development of Career Intensity. The techniques of persuasion—of helping convince people to believe in you—are critical to your success. The first step in the sales process—for both Intrepreneurs and Entrepreneurs—is to sell yourself. Once people believe in you, they will believe that you can help them and their business.

Chapter Ten

MAXIMIZE YOUR CAREER VALUE

The driving force behind this book—the theme of it—is that you have the ability to control your career destiny. You control everything about your employment future.

Think about whether the job you have now matches the dream you had for your career. If it isn't, you're in the half of the working population who is dissatisfied with their current job. Like hundreds of thousands of others, you are prone to tunnel vision when it comes to your career. You may believe that, if you've worked in a certain industry for a significant length of time, your qualifications only allow you to hold another position in the same industry—or even in a certain segment of that industry. Your mind cannot picture breaking out of that box.

OTHERS CAN'T JUDGE YOUR VALUE

Sometimes, your superiors instill in you a mindset that is set in stone. You sit through performance review after performance review and hear feedback that tells you that you need to improve in a certain area. This immediately translates into a perception that you are deficient in that area, and that area is critical to your success in moving into the next position. You are wrong to accept this feedback as gospel.

There are four reasons why the feedback you receive on your performance review isn't the best way to judge your overall value:

Performance review feedback is subjective. A
performance review reflects the opinion of one person.

Although some companies use a 360-degree feedback tool that includes feedback from peers and subordinates under the guise of objectivity, this just offers subjectivity in greater volume. In many cases, performance reviews are a popularity contest.

Guidelines often prevent true value assessment. Your supervisor has specific guidelines that she has to follow when she completes your review. Her feedback will be confined to, or at least influenced by, the company's guidelines. Helpful individual feedback can be restricted by the rules in place for completing the process.

The company sets the success criteria. You are evaluated based upon a conglomeration of criteria that may not exist in any one person. If your company has put thought into the development of its performance management system, it has probably developed specific criteria to evaluate individual performance. This criterion is often based upon qualities that exist in their best performers or in a cross-section of these individuals. No one may be able to become the super-employee who receives the highest performance evaluation.

True measurement is rare. Very few companies have true measures of individual performance that are helpful in assessing value. Companies that rely on individual sales performance to drive growth may have some degree of measurement in place. What they do with that measurement is another story. It is difficult to find an organization that associates "hard" metrics with individual performance evaluation. When you do find a company that does so, it often accepts the numbers at face value. It does not look at the supporting factors that influence individual performance. You become the number you produce.

Remember the Individual Economy

As we discussed at the beginning of this book, we are now faced with an Individual Economy—a system where the productivity of every single person is important to the success of the company. We've reviewed strategies that you can implement to leverage this focus on individual performance in order to improve your career. The problem you face is that the evaluation systems of most organizations are not very good at measuring or evaluating your performance.

What is an aggressive Intrepreneur to do? How can she make certain that the value that she has created and promoted—as described in this book—is recognized? Unfortunately, the culture and the norms of each organization so vastly differ that it would be impossible to standardize a measurement to help identify value. The forms that your supervisor fills out and sends in to Human Resources are not indicative of who you really are. They are not even indicative of the actual work you have done during a set time period. They are essentially one person's opinion of your performance. This person only has importance to you in the workplace.

Too many people allow their futures to be determined by what one individual has written about them on a standardized form. Too many people feel that they are beholden to their annual performance review process in determining their future. At the most, your performance evaluation is only a valuation of your career in relation to that role. If you receive a mediocre evaluation, does that mean that you will be mediocre in every other position within that company? Absolutely not! You may be an outstanding value creator in another role. Unfortunately, most companies are not set up to allow you to try on jobs for a good fit like you would try on a pair of pants.

This leaves the determination of the right role up to you. No one else can or should assume this responsibility. How can you tell when you are working in a field that is truly a good fit for you? Here are some key indicators:

> **You look forward to going to work.** The substance of what you do energizes you. The actual work of your job is fun or rewarding. There are some days when you actually think to yourself, "I can't believe I get paid to do this."
> **You become emotional when you describe your work to other people.** Your passion is evident even in the most

mundane conversation. People can sense the energy
coming off of you as you describe something that
happened during your workday.

Time flies. This is not just true when you are having fun. It
is also true when you are doing something that is truly a
good match for your talent, skills, and knowledge. You
get to work and settle in and, before you know it, it's
time to go home.

It's easy to find people you care about through your job.
When you are in an environment that makes you feel
good about yourself, you tend to be less guarded. This
often allows you to open up and share personal
information about yourself with your coworkers. More
often than not, this leads to close friendships and other
bonding experiences.

All of these characteristics can be true of both successful Entrepreneurs and Intrepreneurs. They are especially evident among
people who own their own businesses. As one of my friends who
owns a technology company put it, "I may not know what tomorrow will bring, but I definitely know that I won't ever have to
work with a jerk again." This is the biggest advantage of going out
on your own and starting a business. You do not have to worry
about the people who make up your company. You control all of
those decisions.

This brings us back to the question of overall value. How do
you know if you are making the kind of money you should be making in a job? For years, organizations have looked to the local market to help them set wage scales. I've been involved in many
exercises where companies survey the local market to set a minimum, midpoint, and maximum compensation level for each position. Many companies have lost outstanding value creators because
they were at the maximum allowable salary for their position.

I suggest a new wage scale. This one will be based upon the
market for the value you create. How much would you be worth if
you were to start your own business and go out and sell what you
had to offer? To answer this question, you need only find someone

who is doing what you do and is doing it in his own business. Even if you have a complementary or a support skill, you are providing value and you should be able to market what you have to offer. Do your own competitive analysis. The results are not for your employer. They are for you. Only you can decide if it is worthwhile to stay where you are or seek other opportunities. The best way to evaluate your performance is to understand the value you provide to the company. As I meet with and discuss career advancement with successful individuals, I find that many of them do not understand the value they provide to their organizations. The best way to test this value is to look at what your talent and skill would be worth if you set up your own shop. Discount this by the amount of tolerance you have for risk—because entrepreneurship is a risky proposition—and determine if you can live with the discount your current company is receiving on your overall value.

FOCUS ON VALUE CREATION

To positively influence your career, you must continuously improve the amount of value you provide to your clients—your customers and the people with whom you work. But providing value is only half of the success formula on the value side of the Career Intensity Matrix. You must also demonstrate the value that you provide by marketing your services.

Value creation comes from the use of your talent combined with the skills and knowledge you have acquired through experience. Your goal should be to master your craft in each position you hold. Oftentimes, these positions require deep, industry-specific (or even job-specific) knowledge. A requirement for deep specialization will, as an Intrepreneur, automatically increase your value to your employer or, as an Entrepreneur, to your customers.

Although becoming a specialist is an excellent way to increase your value within a company, it will often limit your ability to move from one organization to another. In addition, specialists face the risk of being replaced by technological solutions designed to improve efficiency. Intrepreneurs who use specialization to drive their value should make certain that their area of expertise will be necessary as the organization evolves. In addition, a specialist Intrepreneur should practice continuous improvement related to his specialty. Attending seminars, attending workshops, and acquiring certifications are the best way to keep your skills up-to-date.

There are some universal drivers of career value upon which all Workplace Warriors or Management Mavericks who aspire to be successful Entrepreneurs or Intrepreneurs should focus. We have touched upon some of these drivers in this book. They include being persistent (Chapter One); adopting a strategic mindset (Chapter Three); developing and working toward meaningful goals (Chapter Four); and using preparation to take advantage of opportunity (Chapter Six).

These are the basics of value creation for both Entrepreneurs and Intrepreneurs. If you focus on and master these key drivers, you will become valuable to your company and to your clients. Although these basics will take you a long way—the continuous improvement process you have begun by picking up this book will demand more from you—your internal drive will require that you move beyond basic value creation. This is the point where you will find the greatest opportunity. For example, as an Entrepreneur who has mastered the basics of value creation, you may consider expanding your business into other locations—or even franchising your business to others. The ultimate dream for many Entrepreneurs who are advanced value creators is to take the business public (list stock for sale or a major exchange). An Intrepreneur who is an advanced value creator will move through the ranks of middle management and position herself for a leadership role in the organization.

The critical component necessary for driving advanced value creation is creating a team of experts who will help advise you as you advance through your career. These experts will serve as your own personal board of directors. This personal board does not need to hold formal meetings. It can simply be individuals who offer you advice on how you can work to continuously improve the value you provide to your clients. The board can incorporate friends, relatives, or professional contacts—such as doctors, lawyers, or accountants. Their areas of expertise can vary, but you should require brutal honesty from all of them. These are not roles you want filled by "yes men."

As we have discussed, creating value is only half of the value side of the Career Intensity Matrix. The other half is demonstrating and promoting the value that you provide. We have discussed the basics of developing your personal brand in Chapter Seven. Then we moved into leveraging your brand and activities to build a web of advocates that will help get the word out about the extraordinary value you provide (Chapter Eight). Finally, we discussed how you could pitch your ideas to others in ways that will help them be more receptive to your message (Chapter Nine).

These drivers of value perception will serve you well during your entire career. They will ensure that the world is aware of who you are and the value you provide. Intrepreneurs will find themselves revisiting both the overall strategy and the specific tactics of value perception time and again. As an Intrepreneur, it is easy to become swept away in the process of *creating* value. Your focus often results in neglecting the *demonstration* or *promotion* of the value you create. Additionally, Intrepreneurs often view self-promotion in a negative light. Most often, this is a perception generated by those who do not create value themselves. You must ignore these people. The only person you can count on to promote you is you. You must share your good work with the world.

Entrepreneurs have a unique challenge related to value demonstration. You must focus diligently on simultaneously creating and demonstrating value. There are very few people who can master these two critical disciplines effectively. The Entrepreneur must decide upon which aspect of the value side of the Career Intensity Matrix he would like to focus, and then he must seek help with the other aspect. If you are an Entrepreneur who is passionate about developing products and services, you must hire someone who will be your marketing alter ego. Likewise, if you are a marketing genius, hire an operations expert to help you refine the development of your products or services. This is one of the critical components of success as an Entrepreneur.

Everyone should work to improve his or her tolerance for risk. In reality, though, this is a misnomer. Superachievers shift their perception of risk and often believe that the greatest risk is in missing an opportunity. It is the goal of every Entrepreneur and Intrepreneur to get to this point in her relationship with the unknown. By its very nature, the word "risk" causes many people to shut down. When they hear it, they immediately fear the worst. To most, risk symbolizes loss. They do not see the potential associated with taking advantage of opportunity. This is why I elected to embed some of the basics of risk tolerance development into different areas of this book. It is my hope that you have made the shift from a perception of risk as a loss to a perception of risk as an opportunity as you look at this side of the Career Intensity Matrix.

In order to help you capitalize on opportunity, reflect on the topics of facing fear, mental training, and acting "as if' (Chapter Two). Strategic thinking, managing emotions, and planning for contingencies (Chapter Three) will help increase your confidence. Working towards your goals (Chapter Four) will help you build the momentum necessary to steamroll any risk associated with your career desires. Chapter Five has information on eliminating the risk of doing nothing, listing proactive steps that will influence the outcome of each event, and avoiding assumptions to reduce risk. Finally, Chapter Six describes specific preparation methods that will help you gain confidence in every encounter. This confidence will immediately increase your desire to capitalize on opportunities.

At the end of any book or training program, there is often the opportunity to look back and reflect upon what you have learned. In many instances, a sense of melancholy will set in, along with a feeling of accomplishment. One of the best ways I have found to combat the sense of sadness that comes with the ending of a learning experience is to view it as the beginning of something better. In this case, the end of this book is truly the beginning of a better career.

Remember that it is *your* career. Many of us—myself, your personal board of directors, and your family—are here for you as resources that you can call upon at any time. Ultimately, it is your career, and you must take charge of it. Create value, capitalize on opportunity, and always let the world know how great you truly are!

Resources

TOOLS TO INCREASE YOUR CAREER INTENSITY

Reading this book was just the beginning of a career-changing relationship. There are a number of resources available to you at www.careerintensity.com. Some of the valuable tools you can use to help manage your career are highlighted in the information that follows:

The Career Intensity Blog—This daily infusion of insight from Dave Lorenzo is sure to keep the ideas contained in this book fresh in your mind.

The Career Intensity Executive Briefing Audio Series—This comprehensive collection of compact discs allow you to immerse yourself in the detail of creating and improving the value you provide to your customers.

The Career Intensity Executive Briefing Video Collection— This collection of educational sessions featuring Dave Lorenzo breaks down the key value drivers of intense careers. Topics include Strategic Planning and Decision Making; Goal Setting; Personal Due Diligence; Individual Brand Management; Personal Marketing; Persuasion and Influence; and many more.

The Career Intensity E-Book—This electronic version of Career Intensity includes links to Web-based resources. These resources are updated regularly and provide point-and-click access to the latest sites that can help those who are looking to improve in their current role, looking to move into a new role, or are looking to start their own business.

The Career Intensity Newsletter—An exclusive members-only electronic magazine, the Career Intensity Newsletter provides readers with an insider's look at the careers of the most successful superachievers. Packed with tips and insights that can't be found anywhere else, this is a must-read for those who are serious about success—and it's delivered right to your inbox each month.

Personal Strategy Coaching—Dave Lorenzo and his team are always available to help you increase your Career Intensity and achieve your goals. There are only a limited number of personal coaching opportunities available and the screening process is rigorous. If you are interested in being considered for this elite program, please complete the online application at www.careerintensity.com.

Career Intensity Seminars—Dave Lorenzo conducts a number of Career Intensity seminars and workshops around the world. Please visit www.careerintensity.com for his complete schedule.

Speaking Engagements—Dave Lorenzo is available as a keynote speaker for groups of all sizes. Additional details are available at www.careerintensity.com.

RECOMMENDED READING

Badaracco, Joseph. *Leading Quietly: An Unorthodox Guide to Doing the Right Thing.* Harvard Business School Press, 2002.

Bell, Chip R. *Customers As Partners: Building Relationships That Last.* Berrett-Koehler Publishers, 1994.

Benton, D. A. *How to Think Like a CEO: The 22 Vital Traits You Need to Be the Person at the Top.* Warner Books, 1999.

Buckingham, Marcus, and Curt Coffman. *First, Break All the Rules: What the World's Greatest Managers Do Differently.* Simon & Schuster, 1999.

Buckingham, Marcus, and Donald O. Clifton. *Now, Discover Your Strengths.* Free Press, 2001.

Camp, Jim. *Start with NO . . . The Negotiating Tools that the Pros Don't Want You to Know.* Crown Business, 2002.

Carnegie, Dale. *How to Win Friends and Influence People* (Reissued edition). Pocket Books, 1990.

Chu, Chin-Ning. *Thick Face, Black Heart: The Asian Path to Thriving, Winning and Succeeding.* Nicholas Brealey Publishing, 1995.

Cialdini, Robert B. *Influence: The Psychology of Persuasion* (Revised). Collins, 1998.

Dinkin, Greg. *The Poker MBA: Winning in Business No Matter What Cards You're Dealt.* Crown Business, 2002.

Dixit, Avinash K., and Barry Nalebuff. *Thinking Strategically: The Competitive Edge in Business, Politics, and Everyday Life* (Revised). W.W. Norton & Company, 1993.

Farber, Steve. *The Radical Leap: A Personal Lesson in Extreme Leadership.* Chicago: Dearborn Trade, 2004.

Ferrazzi, Keith, and Tahl Raz. *Never Eat Alone: And Other Secrets to Success, One Relationship at a Time.* Currency, 2005.

Fisher, Roger, William Ury, and Bruce Patton. *Getting to Yes: Negotiating Agreement Without Giving In* (Second edition). Penguin, 1991.

Fox, Jeffrey J. *How to Become CEO: The Rules for Rising to the Top of Any Organization.* Hyperion, 1998.

Gladwell, Malcom. *The Tipping Point: How Little Things Can Make a Big Difference.* Little, Brown, 2000.

Godin, Seth. *Free Prize Inside: The Next Big Marketing Idea.* Portfolio, 2004.

Godin, Seth. *Purple Cow: Transform Your Business by Being Remarkable.* Portfolio, 2003.

Greene, Robert, and Joost Elffers. *The 48 Laws of Power.* Penguin, 2000.

Greene, Robert. *The Art of Seduction* (Reprint). Penguin, 2003.

Hill, Napoleon. *Think and Grow Rich* (Reissued edition). Ballantine Books, 1987.

Jansen, Julie. *I Don't Know What I Want, But I Know It's Not This: A Step-by-Step Guide to Finding Gratifying Work.* Penguin, 2003.

Johnson, C. Ray. *CEO Logic: How to Think and Act Like a Chief Executive*. Career Press, 1998.

Koch, Richard. *The 80/20 Principle: The Secret to Success by Achieving More with Less*. Currency, 1999.

Mackay, Harvey. *Swim with the Sharks Without Being Eaten Alive: Outsell, Outmanage, Outmotivate and Outnegotiate Your Competition*. Collins, 2005.

Maister, David H., Charles H. Green, and Robert M. Galford. *The Trusted Advisor*. Free Press, 2001.

McCormack, Mark H. *What They Don't Teach You at Harvard Business School: Notes from a Street-Smart Executive* (Reissued edition). Bantam Books, 1986.

Moltz, Barry. *You Need to Be a Little Crazy: The Truth About Starting and Growing Your Business*. Kaplan Publishing, 2003.

Nutt, Paul C. *Why Decisions Fail: Avoiding the Blunders and Traps that Lead to Debacles*. Berrett-Koehler Publishers, 2002.

Peters, Tom. *Re-imagine! Business Excellence in a Disruptive Age*. DK Publishing, 2003.

Pink, Daniel H. *Free Agent Nation: How America's Independent Workers Are Transforming the Way We Live*. Warner Books, 2001.

Rath, Tom, and Clifton, Donald O. *How Full Is Your Bucket? Positive Strategies for Work and Life*. Gallup Press, 2004.

Ries, Al, and Ries Laura. *The 22 Immutable Laws of Branding*. Collins, 2002.

Rosen, Emanuel. *The Anatomy of Buzz: How to Create Word of Mouth Marketing*. Currency, 2002.

Seligman, Martin E. P. *Authentic Happiness: Using the New Positive Psychology to Realize Your Potential for Lasting Fulfillment.* Free Press, 2004.

Smith, Benson, and Tony Rutigliano. *Discover Your Sales Strengths: How the World's Greatest Salespeople Develop Winning Careers.* Warner Business Books, 2003.

Trout, Jack. *Differentiate or Die: Survival in Our Era of Killer Competition.* Wiley, 2000.

GLOSSARY

The 3–9–27 Pyramid: A goal-setting methodology that employs three tiers and is comprised of three long-term (ten-year) Overarching Goals; nine medium-term (one-year) Contributory Goals; and 27 weekly Action Items. The third-tier Action Items support the second-tier Contributory Goals, which, in turn, support the first-tier Overarching Goals.

The 80/20 Rule: Originally developed by economist Vilfredo Pareto, the underlying theory is that a few (20 percent) are vital and many (80 percent) are trivial. In business, applying the most effort to the vital 20 percent of a given project generates greater results.

Affirmation: A positive phrase that is often repeated in order to reprogram the subconscious mind and eliminate negative self-talk, such as, "I am a good person."

"As If" Thinking: Leveraging your imagination to reach your goals by envisioning your success before it happens.

BOAST: An acronym for making goals actionable that stands for Bold, Open, Achievement, Significant, and Transformation.

Boiling the Ocean: This means conducting too much analysis of a situation. People who boil the ocean tend to become paralyzed by the amount of information they possess. This creates difficulty in decision making.

Boosters: Individuals who share their experiences broadly through a platform that allows them to reach mass audiences. They can amplify your personal brand in both volume and stature.

"By-the-Way" Technique: This is a technique used to leave behind one last piece of information or extract one last fact from a client or prospective client. As you leave the interaction, you turn and say "by the way . . ." and introduce your information or ask your question.

Career Intensity: The drive for continuous individual improvement that is the hallmark of successful entrepreneurs and top corporate executives.

Coke Effect: This is a term used to describe how the perception of scarcity can increase demand. It is derived from the story of "Old Coke" being pulled from the market in 1985.

Cycle of Continuous Career Improvement: The process of conducting a personal situation analysis, creating value, and demonstrating value. This is an ongoing system that superachievers use to improve their value throughout their career.

Dimensions of Credibility: The qualities that make one believable and trustworthy, namely: expertise; goodwill; dynamic energy; and sociability.

Direct Persuasion: Using a well-reasoned argument, usually supported by data, to sell an idea, service, or product. The four elements of direct persuasion are position, problem, possibilities, and proposal.

Entrepreneurs: People who have high-risk tolerance, tremendous confidence in themselves and their teams, and who create tremendous value for their customers. They have the ability to change or disrupt entire industries, either locally or globally.

FEAR: The acronym for False Evidence Appearing Real.

Five Factors: The elements that influence strategic thinking, namely, time, control, experience, the unknown, and outcome finality.

Five Irrational Fears: Concerns that prevent people from realizing their career goals, namely fear of the unknown, fear of failure, fear of commitment, fear of disapproval, and fear of success.

Five Ps of Personal Branding: Five personal qualities that are essential to the success of a personal brand, namely, patience, proof, passion, persistence, and perception.

Indirect Persuasion: Using peripheral information and cues from the listener, rather than a well-reasoned argument, to sell an idea, service, or product.

Individual Economy: A new business model whereby the value created by an individual becomes personal equity and trumps the traditional loyalty exhibited by companies toward their employees and vice versa.

Intrepreneurs: Employees who engage in the drive for continuous individual improvement and create enormous value within a corporate setting.

The Lucky Seven: Story narratives that are embraced by the media, retold by repeaters, and mentioned by boosters, namely: Sex, Lies, and the Outrageous; The Who-Dun-It; The Hype; The Cinderella Story; The Hilarious; The Hero; and The Secrets.

Management Mavericks: Employees, often perceived as rogues, who embrace risk and tend to move forward and implement solutions without the support of their internal and external customers.

Mental Training: The process of developing mental toughness by challenging yourself with completing increasingly difficult tasks that require you to be alone.

Outcome-Driven Thinking: The process of entering into each interaction with a desired result.

Personal Brand: The perception of you in the minds of your customers.

Repeaters: Individuals who share their experiences broadly throughout their communities. They are essential to generating buzz about the value of your product or service through word of mouth.

Rules of the Road: Precepts to follow to preserve your personal brand when interacting with customers, namely: believe in yourself; keep your dealings moral, ethical, and legal; follow The Golden Rule; allow the other person to leave with their dignity intact; and allow others to take credit for great ideas.

SMART Goals: A goal-setting acronym that stands for Specific, Measurable, Achievable, Realistic, and Tangible.

Starbucks Moments: This describes a moment of meaningful interaction while waiting for a drink to be prepared at a Starbucks Coffee Bar.

Starbucks Speech: This is the short script you have prepared when you run into someone you would like to meet as you wait for your drink to be prepared in a Starbucks Coffee Bar.

Starbucks Stalker: This is someone who hangs around a Starbucks Coffee Bar with the hope of meeting someone influential.

Strategic Thinking: A distinct perspective that helps you break down complicated processes into easily manageable pieces that can be arranged to present a clear set of alternatives.

Superachiever: A person whose performance exceeds the norm by a wide margin.

Three Lies of Career Limitation: Falsehoods related to security, work benefits and loyalty that employees tell themselves to justify maintaining the status quo of their careers.

Three Rules of Engagement: The philosophy followed by people with Career Intensity in their interactions with others: know yourself; investigate your target; and define and execute a plan of attack for every meeting.

Value Creators: Aggressive, passionate individuals who are committed to the success of their careers. Their actions are swift and bold. They are decisive and driven to achieve. They are creative and calculating. They combine skills, knowledge, and talent with specific strategies that become the Career Intensity that propels them to success.

Workplace Warriors: The backbone of large organizations, these employees follow orders and measure their worth by the clock, rather than by their accomplishments and growth. They are risk-adverse and do not create individual value.

ACKNOWLEDGMENTS

It is impossible to thank everyone with whom I have worked during the past twenty years, yet all of those individuals had a hand in the development of the content of this book.

My work ethic, loyalty, and intense competitive spirit come from my father—Vince Lorenzo. My emotional investment in everything I do and my intellectual curiosity comes from my mother—Rosemary Lorenzo. I am truly grateful for their guidance and love.

My sister and brother-in-law, Laura and Brian Baiker, have been incredibly supportive and enthusiastic in this process. I deeply appreciate their insight and their friendship.

I am fortunate to work with (and be related to) John Ackerina. He has selflessly given his time, energy, and expertise to this project, and I cannot thank him enough for his efforts.

There is nothing more comforting during times of career uncertainty then a conversation with a good friend. I'm fortunate to have a group of fantastic friends who offer great objective advice mixed in with a healthy dose of humor. To Pat Murphy, Rob Jacapraro, Scott Brennan, Brian Bartkus, and Philip Zmuda, I say, thanks for hanging in there with me.

Special thanks goes to Joe Vetromile, who helped me organize the initial thoughts that eventually became this book. I also am deeply appreciative of the efforts of Sally Smith, a terrific editor. Andrea Leonarz has been a good friend as well as a tenacious marketing advisor, and I'm grateful for her help.

Several people reviewed the manuscript in its various forms. The feedback I received was invaluable. Thanks to Ingrid Clavijo,

Josh Shaub, Julia Phelps, Irena Briganti, Liz Howekamp, Dave Every, Brian Murphy, and Tracy and Michael Parrillo.

I have learned a lot about entrepreneurship from Manny (Eddie) and Maria Lorenzo. I'm thankful that they have become a big part of my life, and I look forward to continuing to learn from their success.

I'm also grateful to Cata and Martha Martillo for their support and affection. One day we will all be sitting in Martha's restaurant talking about this book while we enjoy a great pork sandwich.

Thanks to Josephine Cheda and her beautiful girls, Angela and Angelica, for brightening my weekends. After spending hours staring at a computer screen, it is always refreshing to run around the house and eat lots of chocolate.

Over the past four years, Kathalina Nunez has become a second sister to me and I am grateful for her support, her friendship, and her sense of humor.

Finally, I say thanks to Kary Cheda. She has been my partner on this project and in my life for the past four years. The true secret to my Career Intensity comes from the strength she gives me. I thank God every day that she is a part of my life.

INDEX

ORDER FORM

Additional copies of *Career Intensity: Business Strategy for Workplace Warriors and Entrepreneurs* can be found at your local bookstore.

Copies are also available at special quantity discounts for sales promotions, employee premiums, or educational purposes. Please contact the publisher at orders@ogmanpr.com to order.

You can also order books at www.careerintensity.com or fill out the following form and mail or fax it to:

Ogman Press, Inc
217 East 85th Street
Box 170
New York, NY 10028
Fax: 212-327-2371

Please send _____ copies of **Career Intensity** @ $29.95 each

Name _____

Company _____

Address _____

City _____ **State** _____ **Zip** _____

Phone Number _____

Fax Number _____

E-mail _____

Credit Card # _____

Expiration Date _____

Security Code (three or four digit number on back of card) _____

Please include $4 for shipping and handling. New York State orders must add 8.75% sales tax.